"Each day when I move out into the world, I want to be clothed with the truths shared in *Slow Kingdom Coming*. I'm not, but I want to be. I want to be as gentle and as smart as Kent is as he writes. I want to be as opened-eyed and open-hearted as those he quotes, from Weil and Bonhoeffer to a homeless vet in a dark park and a young mom praying over a photo on her refrigerator. I'll recommend [this] to everyone I know who wants to do justice more wisely and love mercy more purely and walk ever more humbly with our God. Yes, I love this book!"
Lynne Hybels, advocate for global engagement, Willow Creek Community Church

"Kent Annan is doing some of the most redemptive work on the planet. His newest book is a breath of fresh air—he steps back from all the action to consider the practices, prayer and disciplined reflection that sustains the work of justice. *Slow Kingdom Coming* is about going slow in a fast world, going deep in a shallow world and going far in a world that likes shortcuts. Brilliant."
Shane Claiborne, speaker, activist, author of *Executing Grace*

"There is an African proverb that says, 'If you want to go fast, go alone; if you want to go far, go together.' In *Slow Kingdom Coming* Kent Annan shows us how to live into the meaning of these words by experiencing the life-changing impact of working together for justice and healing, both locally and globally. If you want to be a part of the change you hope to see in the world, I highly recommend this book!"
Brenda Salter McNeil, author of *A Credible Witness* and *Roadmap to Reconciliation*

"Seeking first the kingdom of God often feels like running the last mile of a marathon in wet sand. Progress seems painfully slow, and we often want to cry out in agony. Kent Annan provides us with practices to give us strength in the race so we can run and not grow weary. I wish I'd had this book years ago!"
Brian Fikkert, coauthor of *When Helping Hurts*

"*Slow Kingdom Coming* is one of the most honest yet hopeful reads for those who seek to do the work of justice today. Kent calls out shortsighted, quick-fix approaches and then offers a more responsible, sustainable way to love the world. This book is accessible, inspiring and actionable. It should be required reading for anyone who is serious about participating in the slow yet beautiful work of God's redemption in the world."
Jena Lee Nardella, cofounder, Blood:Water, author of *One Thousand Wells*

"*Slow Kingdom Coming* is a siren call, drawing our attention away from a world of quick fixes to God's timing, tempo and purpose. In it Annan graciously gifts us with a deeply practical manual for how to join God at his pace in his work of bringing justice to the time and place we occupy. But more so, he leaves us with an offering of spiritual disciplines by which God can change us more permanently in all areas of our lives. If you want justice, and you want it as God wants it—when God wants it—this is a must-read book."
Curt Thompson, author of *The Soul of Shame*

"An immensely helpful, honest and practical guide for transforming good intentions into tangible action! *Slow Kingdom Coming* gives an honest look at the challenges and shortcuts that accompany a passion for justice."
Nikki Toyama-Szeto, director, International Justice Mission's Institute for Biblical Justice, coauthor of *God of Justice*

"Kent Annan beautifully describes five practices that lead to lasting change and draw us deeper into God's 'slow kingdom coming,' the flourishing life God intends for all creation. This is a fundamentally hopeful vision. If we are attentive to it, it could radically transform how we care for our neighbors—and transform us at the same time."
C. Christopher Smith and John Pattison, authors of *Slow Church*

"In a culture that's tempted by quick and glamorous results, we often forget that the work of mercy and justice is long, laborious and often messy. I deeply appreciated *Slow Kingdom Coming* by Kent Annan because it's vulnerable, confessional and invitational. . . . We need this kind of honesty and truth telling."
Eugene Cho, founder, One Day's Wages, and author of *Overrated*

"This beautiful book will help you find that sweet spot, that healing way of life, and keep you living there so you can join God in the slow kingdom coming."
Brian D. McLaren, author, speaker, activist

"If you care about making the world a better place, this is an important book for examining your motivations and learning to cooperate with the Divine in the healing of our world."
Phileena Heuertz, author of *Pilgrimage of a Soul*

"We all get discouraged, impatient and diverted by ordinary approaches to helping. This book teaches us core spiritual practices that will result in a steady dedication to God and to his care for the vulnerable. . . . To anyone with a heart for justice but some confusion when it comes to practicing compassion, I highly recommend this book!"
Joel C. Hunter, senior pastor, Northland: A Church Distributed

"I had three reasons for reading *Slow Kingdom Coming*: I am on my own spiritual journey and find Kent's writing inspiring. My writing includes lots of stories and Kent is a master story writer. And finally, I serve on my church's mission committee and we greatly need the frame Kent provides here. Kent is a gifted writer with important and timely things to share in this book."
Stephen Lundin, bestselling author of *Fish! A Remarkable Way to Boost Morale and Improve Performance*

"If you've ever found long-term service and loving your neighbor to be more difficult than you initially imagined, then you need to read *Slow Kingdom Coming*. . . . Grounded in real life experience and rooted in Scripture, this is a book I will be widely sharing with my global colleagues and friends."
Peter Greer, president and CEO, HOPE International, coauthor of *Mission Drift*

"*Slow Kingdom Coming* is deeply truthful and beautifully rendered, with stories drawn from the lives of colaborers around the world alongside important research. . . . This book deserves a close read by all those drawn to live out Scripture's commands to do justice in our broken world."
Brian Howell, professor of anthropology, Wheaton College, author of *Short-Term Mission*

SLOW KINGDOM COMING

PRACTICES FOR DOING JUSTICE, LOVING MERCY AND WALKING HUMBLY IN THE WORLD

KENT ANNAN

IVP Books

An imprint of InterVarsity Press
Downers Grove, Illinois

InterVarsity Press
P.O. Box 1400
Downers Grove, IL 60515-1426
ivpress.com
email@ivpress.com

InterVarsity Press® is the book-publishing division of InterVarsity Christian Fellowship/USA®, a movement of students and faculty active on campus at hundreds of universities, colleges and schools of nursing in the United States of America, and a member movement of the International Fellowship of Evangelical Students. For information about local and regional activities, visit intervarsity.org.

Scripture quotations, unless otherwise noted, are from the New Revised Standard Version of the Bible, copyright 1989 by the Division of Christian Education of the National Council of the Churches of Christ in the USA. Used by permission. All rights reserved.

Published in association with Creative Trust Literary Group, 210 Jamestown Park, Suite 200, Brentwood, Tennessee, 37027, creativetrust.com.

While any stories in this book are true, some names and identifying information may have been changed to protect the privacy of individuals.

Cover design: Cindy Kiple
Interior design: Beth McGill
Images: cloudscape: Vadmary/iStockphoto
        rusty billboard: Bart Sadowski/iStockphoto
        trinity icon: © Lehakok/Dreamstime.com—Mosaic Gate Icon Old Testament Trinity,
        Designed by E. Klimov and made in 1942 in Germany; photo

ISBN 978-0-8308-4455-5 (print)
ISBN 978-0-8308-9998-2 (digital)

Printed in the United States of America ∞

Library of Congress Cataloging-in-Publication Data

Names: Annan, Kent, 1973- author.

Title: Slow kingdom coming : practices for doing justice, loving mercy, and walking humbly in the world / Kent Annan.

Description: Downers Grove : InterVarsity Press, 2016. | Includes bibliographical references.

Identifiers: LCCN 2016005170 | ISBN 9780830844555 (pbk. : alk. paper)

Subjects: LCSH: Christianity and justice. | Church work.

Classification: LCC BR115.J8 A55 2016 | DDC 261.8--dc23

LC record available at http://lccn.loc.gov/2016005170

| P | 25 | 24 | 23 | 22 | 21 | 20 | 19 | 18 | 17 | 16 | 15 | 14 | 13 | 12 | 11 | 10 | 9 | 8 | 7 | 6 | 5 | 4 | 3 | 2 | 1 |
| Y | 34 | 33 | 32 | 31 | 30 | 29 | 28 | 27 | 26 | 25 | 24 | 23 | 22 | 21 | 20 | 19 | 18 | 17 | 16 |

He is not, therefore, eternally responsible for whether he reaches his goal within this world of time. But without exception, he is eternally responsible for the kind of means he uses.

And when he . . . only uses those means which are genuinely good, then, in the judgment of eternity, he is at the goal.

SØREN KIERKEGAARD, *PURITY OF HEART IS TO WILL ONE THING*

CONTENTS

PREFACE

Over the past twenty years I've personally and professionally succumbed to various failed justice shortcuts instead of living the freedom of faithful practices. I've been paralyzed by the complexity of trying to help others. I've huddled in bed during daylight because of sadness and discouragement. I've rushed to get good things done and so didn't treat people as well as I should. I'm still confessing regularly my faults and my longing to better participate in justice—that God's kingdom would come on earth as in heaven. I confess that I wish this weren't such a slow kingdom coming.

But I've also seen people be incredibly generous with their time, talents and money in ways that inspire about humanity and are testimonies to God's love. I've seen people in brutal circumstances make the best of new opportunities. I've seen hope stay tenaciously alive when by almost any measure it should be dead. I've seen ingenuity and humility in service of love.

All this has happened as I've been working for justice through education in Haiti for the past thirteen years. I've also been teaching and speaking around the United States and Canada. Before this I worked for a couple of years with refugees in Europe. I've been on short-term missions trips and have led some. I've had the photo of a sponsored child on my fridge. I've worked for and been a director of nonprofits. I'm a small donor and also a board member of a foundation that gives away millions of dollars each year.

Out of these experiences I've written this book about doing good without hiding from the bad—both around us and within us—because we're called to be part of God's kingdom coming. We're invited to confess our vulnerabilities in serving justice so we can avoid dead-end shortcuts that damage others and ourselves. We're invited to accept the grace and responsibility of living into our deepest longings for God's kingdom. We're invited to a responsible approach to helping other people flourish in our neighborhoods and in our world, where there is too much suffering. We're invited to be part of deep, lasting change.

I've been seeking to understand how we can best stay faithfully committed to humbly doing justice and loving mercy in our world. This has led to the five practices in this book. Where can they apply?

These days racial injustice and the threat of climate change are top of mind. No big issues are more important right now, right? Well, except human trafficking and endemic violence against women also must be added to the list. Then there is the growing chasm between the wealthy and poor, with the resulting disenfranchisement and the long-term fracturing of society. The latest refugee crisis. Access to education and clean water. Protecting the rights of people who are vulnerable because of their sexuality. Cruelty toward animals in factory farming. Nuclear disarmament. And the list keeps multiplying all too easily.

And then without even touching that list, think of your daily life. Your neighbor who has emotional issues and is deeply lonely and latches on every chance she gets, but even if you were to give her all the attention you had to give for the rest of your days, you still wouldn't meet her heart-rending, unquenchable need.

So you feel guilty avoiding her as you drive to the grocery store, and then along the way at an intersection stands a man in a tattered, too-heavy coat holding a cardboard sign that says, "Homeless vet, will work for food." And then the sign says, "God bless you."

It's hard to feel God's blessing in this moment. It's tempting to respond with, "Hey God, I'm willing to skip the blessing if we could get a little more help down here—because it's more than we can handle!"

Yes, it is more than we can handle. The five practices in this book can help you find the freedom to handle *what you can* and *what you're called to*—and then handle this *well*—as we respond faithfully to needs and opportunities around us.

PARTICIPATING IN THE COMING KINGDOM

The kingdom of God has come near.

MARK 1:15

On the fifteenth of each month, Alicia has thirty dollars withdrawn from her checking account to sponsor Belyse, a beautiful, brown-eyed girl from Kenya, who then gets school and a hot meal each day. Alicia's job is a grind at the moment. Belyse's photo on her fridge has become deeply important to her, almost like an icon. Pulling out milk for morning coffee, she pauses to quickly pray for Belyse, but also that through Belyse God would give her own life more meaning.

But she's read the small print. She knows her money doesn't all go to Belyse, which makes sense. But it means even this straightforward bond is manipulated. She feels distant from the help she is giving—like she's watching it on TV instead of being part of it. She consumes justice. She picked Belyse by scrolling through photos, like picking a new pair of shoes off Zappos.com. She feels both more connected to and yet further from love because of this relationship.

And then there are the other relationships she has to block out. She lives in Brooklyn, where she works for a tech startup.

Just today she walked up the stairs to her apartment shuffling through junk mail appeals from a wildlife fund, a local domestic abuse shelter, a medical relief organization that works somewhere parched and poor, and a local political group. That's not to mention emails that sneak past her filtering system and urgent Facebook posts from friends. Who can carry this weight of the extinction of a species, abused women around the corner, fixing cleft palates and a political movement to save democracy?

Can I really make a difference? she asks herself. Some of her friends from college did this kind of thing, but they seemed born to organize for fossil-fuel divestment. She was glad they were, but she never saw herself in them. She's looking for herself in Belyse's eyes.

Yet she feels something awakening in her—something like anger mixed with hope—that she is scared and excited to follow. "I don't know if I can do this," she says, "but I know I have to try."

She wants to be free from either ignoring or dragging around the needs of the whole world every day, so she can faithfully do her part.

• • •

Sam's school and city were proud of their focus on tolerance. He is white, and the immediate neighborhood where he lived was mostly white, but the school district was racially and economically diverse. Sam played basketball from the time he was in primary school. On those teams he was usually in the minority. As he got older he sometimes heard his teammates mention racial issues, but the incidents seemed minor, and he and his teammates all shared the same taste in hip-hop.

Then they made it to the varsity team. Sam and his friends got their driver's licenses. Stories of police stops began, but only from the African American players. Other differences followed:

stories of uncles being in jail for minor issues, discrepancies in summer jobs because of family connections. Those jobs then got listed on college applications. The differences didn't break down exactly along color lines, but Sam would have to be colorblind to not see how skin color was a profound factor in all their lives, much more than skin deep. As he grew up, he assumed they all had been living the dream they'd read about in the civil rights part of their history class. His African-American friends had long been awake to the fact that the dream isn't yet here.

Sam recently graduated from college. He's stayed aware, but life became busy. Then Ferguson, New York, Charleston, Black Lives Matter. It's too easy to simply get caught up in taking care of himself, but he knows he wants to care about a lot more.

He wants to stay awake and on guard against the privilege of complacency so he can faithfully learn about and make a difference in a world still marked by racial differences.

• • •

First Church sent a small group to New Orleans right after the hurricane. They worked and prayed and slept on thin mats on the floor. The next year the church went to Uganda to spend time at a camp with former child soldiers. Last year they went to a Guatemalan orphanage. The photos from that trip were especially moving. Next summer they're going to Mexico City. "We feel like we're helping in lots of places," says the young missions pastor, who feels pressure to keep busy people interested, "and it keeps our people engaged!"

It's hard to challenge an approach that is presented so positively, but a few people are asking themselves questions. The trips are starting to feel like flirting, like being a serial dater who moves from girlfriend to girlfriend, bounces from romance to romance. When someone behaves this way in his teens or early twenties, we shake our heads and figure he'll mature. If he keeps flipping through relationships into his thirties or forties, the immaturity starts to look pathological.

Others are saying the trips cost a lot. What about local needs? The young missions pastor knows it's important to connect personally with others who live very different lives. People come back from trips saying, "I feel so grateful for what I have. We shouldn't complain about the little things." That's good to realize, but it's not enough. One week in New Orleans can't touch the deeper racial and economic cracks that burst open after the hurricane. A couple of years later, how are those young men doing in Uganda? Holding babies in Guatemala felt like love, but what did it do for the parents who had to give up their children for adoption? A growing number of people feel uneasy but aren't sure what to do differently.

They want to be free from service that feels self-centered so they can faithfully serve others well.

● ● ●

The four twenty-somethings had been talking about doing something about sex trafficking, but then they are inspired while attending a conference that showed a heartbreaking but warming video about orphans. Orphans in Cambodia need better care; Americans need to adopt more children abandoned into misery.

So they get started. They raise money. They take people on inspiring trips. Tears fall. Prayers reach up. Two of them who had spent a college semester in China move to Cambodia while the other two stay back to start paperwork for a nonprofit and raise money.

Their bold faith inspires people around them. When you're partnering directly with God, why slow down to partner with others? Conversations with people who had already been doing this kind of work were depressing—always about how slow things go—stuck in old-fashioned ways.

Three years later two of the four have quit. They've repeated mistakes they now remember others warning them about. "It's a spiritual battle," they've said in their e-newsletters. "We just have to press on," they tell each other. "Amazing things are happening," they say as they share the before and after photos of how much healthier little Angel has gotten. The gap grows between their story and the reality. Since one of the key Cambodian staff members quit and another was fired for borrowing money from the orphanage budget, well, they're starting to wonder if they're doing as much harm as good. They went on the wings of faith and self-confidence—like those inspiring stories they'd heard. Instead of soaring, they're crashing to earth.

They want to be free from having to be American heroes so they can humbly learn the best faithful ways to help.

• • •

Yanique feels the weight and exhilaration of caring more than the people around her. It started after her family visited a farm when she was eleven and she became a vegetarian. As a teenager she felt like she was climbing from naiveté to cynicism to a more rarified hope. She also felt lonely. After college she spent three days at the original Occupy Wall Street while interning at Amnesty International. Her parents and more conservative friends thought she'd lost it. "She'll get over it" wasn't working anymore to smooth out the frictions.

But her faith also renewed along the way. How she talks about Jesus both disturbs and comforts her mother. When Yanique isn't around, her mom says to her dad, "Honey, she talks about Jesus. She cares about him. Do you know what most of my friends would give for their kids to do that? Won't you be glad she loves Jesus when she has our grandkids one day?"

She wears fair-trade clothes, mostly. She has an iPhone, though she once read about conflict minerals inside it. She wears gray-green hemp slacks that chaff occasionally. She wears TOMS shoes, but then saw the guy sold half the business to venture capitalists for $300 million. Her identity is justice. She supports living-wage legislation, though she barely makes one herself. Her mom thinks Yanique gets life both way more wrong and way more right than she ever has. Yanique's ideals are getting battered. She wonders at times where she ends and her posture begins.

She wants to be free from the confusion about whether she's doing all this to help herself or the people desperately in need so she can faithfully answer God's call.

• • •

This book is about five faithful practices that can help us be committed to deep instead of shallow change. We can be committed to making a long-term difference instead of settling for quick fixes that don't last. When things around us are moving too fast, we can be committed to the slow work of the kingdom. This doesn't mean we want change any less urgently. Quite the opposite. We press forward with a faithful approach because we're so dedicated to hope.

This is especially important as progress in science, technology and information zip around us. People can connect instantly across vast distances. Our knowledge about the far reaches of space and the intricacies of the human body has expanded faster in the past

> **When things around us are moving too fast, we can be committed to the slow work of the kingdom.**

few decades than the previous thousand years. Our phones carry far more computing power than NASA used to put the first people on the moon with Apollo 11. Twelve hours after a news story breaks, experts and hacks around the world have weighed in and everyone has moved on to the next story.

We have free instant access to virtually all the world's information, which was unimaginable thirty years ago. Now I'm annoyed if a bad signal means waiting twenty seconds for a page to load. As the comedian Louis C. K. said about planes, "People say there's delays on flights. Delays, really? New York to California in *five hours.* That used to take *thirty years* to do that and a bunch of you would die on the way there and have a baby. You'd be with a whole different group of people by the time you got there. Now you watch a movie . . . and you're home."[1]

As everything keeps moving faster, we want to upgrade to more speed. Speed begetting speed makes us impatient, feeling ever entitled to more speed.

Yet all of this progress also makes us aware of the world's needs like never before. This same technology means that within hours of his death we can all see the body of a young Syrian refugee boy pulled from the water after he's drowned. We know about disasters around the globe in close to real time. We're aware of so much, yet like the people in the stories at the beginning of this chapter, we don't find making a difference easy. We look to Jesus and find our hope. But looking toward him is also sobering.

Two thousand years ago Jesus prayed, "Thy kingdom come . . . on earth as it is in heaven." We see hopeful signs of and steps toward a better world where love and peace rule, but have to confess the prayer is still a long way from being answered. We're surrounded by a lot of speed these days, but this is a slow kingdom coming.

"Thy kingdom come . . ." but another family huddles in fear as bombs rip through concrete and flesh nearby.

"Thy kingdom come . . ." but another innocent young black man is assaulted as though guilty.

"Thy kingdom come . . ." but another woman was raped on a college campus, her cries later answered with shame instead of justice.

"Thy kingdom come . . ." but it still hadn't come this morning when a child, instead of going to school, walked three miles to fetch a bucket of water that will give him diarrhea.

"Thy kingdom come . . ." but the kingdom is still divided as another person made in God's image was denigrated for her gender or sexuality instead of receiving respect as a fellow child of God.

"Thy kingdom come . . ." while the world's richest eighty-five people luxuriate in as much wealth as the poorest 3.5 billion people try to survive on. Today someone gave everything at his dignity-crushing work to provide for his family. He still didn't bring home enough.

As we watch some things move with so much speed and other things move so slowly, it is important to reflect on how we can stay faithful to doing justice, loving mercy and walking humbly in the world when we want "on earth as it is in heaven" right now.

● ● ●

Sometimes I wish the answer were faster and simpler, like an app with a justice calculator built into my phone or fitness band that would tell me precisely when to give more, what to focus on, when I've done enough and when I'm allowed to pull back. Like a step counter that will say, "10,000 Justice Points Earned Today! You're free from the needs of the world till next week!" But a justice tracker would diminish the truth that we're invited into a *way of life.* Along this way I want to keep following step by step so we can make our way together toward a better kingdom.

Whether considering global issues or a neighbor's need, here's why it sometimes feels like too much to handle:

- *Whose needs?*

   family—friends—neighbors—local—national—international

   women—children—refugees—minorities

- *Respond to disaster or try to prevent it?*

   emergency relief—long-term development—research

- *What level?*

   individuals—institutions—societal systems

   people—animals—environment

- *How to personally get involved?*

   implementer—giver—volunteer

This isn't even an exhaustive grid. No wonder it feels daunting. Yet precisely in the face of this, we still want to help.

This has led me to these practices that can help us stay faithfully committed to doing justice. God calls us collectively and individually to participate in myriad ways in God's kingdom coming on earth. Whatever way you're called, I hope the practices I offer in this book will help you understand *how* to make a more meaningful, lasting difference. I hope they can help you to see more clearly the yeses along the way that make it possible to say the thousand unfortunate nos.

You and I want the kingdom to come, as do the people in the stories that opened this chapter (who are composites of people I've known and heard about). And we rightly want it to get here sooner. Shortcuts can tempt us to settle for an easier-to-reach kingdom that ultimately crumbles. Integrating the right practices will help them—and us—find the freedom to work with determination for lasting change. We can press on with a hope that is both patient and urgent. We're freed to participate in the kingdom coming through these five faithful practices: *attention, confession, respect, partnering* and *truthing*.

> **Shortcuts can tempt us to settle for an easier-to-reach kingdom that ultimately crumbles.**

Whatever your primary vocation, these five practices can help you work faithfully for a world where fewer people suffer and more people flourish. They're related to traditional practices of faithfulness like baptism, Communion, fasting, prayer, tithing and Scripture reading. But we also need specific practices that focus on sustaining us for the mission

> to bring good news to the poor . . .
> to proclaim release to the captives
>   and recovery of sight to the blind,
>   to let the oppressed go free. (Lk 4:18)

These practices are crucial because a paradoxical element of faith within our work for justice is that in a sense we believe the outcomes are completely up to God, yet in another sense it seems God has left the outcomes up to us.

What strikes me, as we begin *Slow Kingdom Coming*, is how these practices also apply to the world of *The Pilgrim's Progress*, which I just began reading with my nine-year-old daughter. Recent bedtime reading had meant my wife and daughter cuddle with youth literature classics that often seemed to lead to their crying together. Meanwhile my son and I just finished the first book of the Harry Potter series and instead of weeping, we seemed to end in wrestling, which, yes, it has been pointed out to me, has the opposite effect of *winding down*.

But after their most recent book, Simone asked my wife if they could read *The Pilgrim's Progress* next because she'd heard about it recently and found a copy on our shelf. I then listened to my wife give my daughter excuses for why they couldn't read it: the language is too archaic; it's too dense. My daughter was unconvinced.

"Actually, now that I think of it," my wife told her, "I'll be honest. I don't like the book and don't want to read it. When I was young and read it, I didn't understand who the different people were and I kept getting tricked into thinking the bad guys were the good guys. And I got tricked into thinking the bad shortcuts were actually a good idea."

This sounded irreverent in a way that made Simone want to read it even more. So she asked if I'd read it with her.

We're twenty-five pages in. It's slow but good. I explain and smooth things out here and there. She's tracking as the main character goes on a quest. He's encouraged to stay on the good path but is soon tempted. He makes a few mistakes and then meets his guide, who questions why he listened to the person who led him off-track: "He bid me with speed get rid of my Burden; and I told him 'twas ease that I sought. . . . So he said that he would show me a better way, and short, not so attended with difficulties as the way, sir, that you set me."[2]

Yes, we're tempted toward the quick and easy way. And why not, since the burden of injustice around us is too much to handle if we try to carry it all? When we commit to faithful practices of justice, we don't shed the burden, but we lighten it enough to continue on the path toward the slow kingdom coming.

We will stumble. We will be tricked by shortcuts. But we learn. We dust ourselves off. We fight bravely to strengthen these practices that help us keep moving forward. The truth is that we're vulnerable, like in *The Pilgrim's Progress*, to being pulled off our path, so it should be hopeful and freeing to admit, yes, we're vulnerable and need guidance.

A few years ago, facing a midlife crisis, or rather hoping to avert one, with a group of friends I did a rigorous twelve-mile obstacle race with twenty-four obstacles.

Beforehand, I looked at what obstacles we might face. Then to get ready I ran a lot of miles. I trained climbing up and over. I did and hated squats. I did monkey bars for the first time in thirty years (a lot harder than they used to be). My children teased me as they showed off how easily they could swing back and forth. When the time came for the race, it was hard but fun. Our team made it to the end. I never would have finished if I had shown up unprepared.

> **We will stumble.**
> **We will be tricked by shortcuts.**
> **But we learn.**

In the work of justice it's also possible to anticipate many of the obstacles we'll face. We can build up endurance in order to keep going when our energy lags. We can build up strength in areas we know we will be tested. I hope and pray the five practices in this book, so much more serious than my running through mud, can inspire and guide your joyful commitment to helping this slow kingdom to come.

For individuals, these five practices apply to how to participate in God's justice in your family, community, country and the world. They can help interactions with a neighbor as well as how to decide what nonprofit to give to. They can help you think through how to volunteer, travel, start a business, buy things. They can become part of the practice of your faith in action, shaping you and shaping the neighborhood and world around you.

For a nonprofit or community group, these practices can help you to align and get focused, to make decisions and grow and learn together. There are always temptations toward mission drift, and it is hard to get different callings to align. None of us can be great at all of these practices; we each have different strengths and vulnerabilities. These practices help to move a group together toward the slow kingdom coming—and to cherish the different gifts and perspectives that each person brings.

For a church, these practices can help you grow and collaborate in ways that transform the lives of those in the church and those you work with as you follow Jesus together. Within a community these practices can help to focus and evaluate your ministries, to encourage people to discover how their gifts fit into working together for justice, and to choose and work with the right partners.

We long to know God, to love God and to be loved by God. Jesus gave the beautiful vision of finishing our life and then hearing from our loving Creator, "Well done, good and faithful servant" (Mt 25:21 NIV). We won't hear these words because we earned them, but, we hope, because we accepted the invitation of grace to participate with God in the kingdom coming. And we can commit to practices that ensure our efforts help others well and also transform our own lives.

Bible scholar Walter Brueggemann says, "The defining ingredient of real human life is fidelity. It's not wealth, power, control, or knowledge. It's fidelity, the question of practice—how do we maintain fidelity [with God]?"[3] The answer isn't easy. *Faithfulness* is both the strength and weakness of Christians as we try to help others. At times our faith that we're doing God's work has led us to sacrificial giving of the highest order of love. But we don't want this same faith to be an excuse to be patronizing or think our good intentions are enough, as though God wouldn't expect us to love our neighbors in the best ways possible.

These practices have sustained me. I've seen the difference they make for people I've watched and worked with, whose stories I share in this book. They can help sustain us for the marathon, because even if there are occasional sprints, this is a lifelong run with regular obstacles. The same love that calls us to work for a more just world also calls for our inner lives to be shaped by justice. Who we are determines how we act, and how we act determines who we are as we do justice, love mercy and walk humbly in the world.

ATTENTION

Awakening to Justice

Remain here, and stay awake with me.

Matthew 26:38

Attention is the purest and rarest form of generosity.

Simone Weil, *Correspondance*

From the outside Calvary Church in Holland, Michigan, looks like a typical large church that many Americans attend. The church developed the typical way: it started small and then began to grow. As the church grew, it had to accommodate worship and programming for hundreds, then more than a thousand people. Which means it needed to build. Which means the congregation has to pay for these buildings. Which means capital campaigns to encourage people to give. For twelve straight years Pastor Frank Wevers led capital campaigns on the $4.5 million project for Calvary, a church of mostly working- and middle-class members.

The good news is they finished phase one of the building project. They were ready to celebrate completing the worship space and retiring their debt by having a mortgage-burning banquet. The bad news is that finishing phase one meant they soon had to start phases two and three of the building plan, which included more space and a Starbucks-like coffee area.

Wevers was tired. The congregation was tired. Yet there was more to do to keep up with the ministry vision. Wevers went on a three-day personal retreat in anticipation of the mortgage-burning banquet. While on the retreat, he started thinking about the biblical idea of jubilee, in which Israel was to rest and reorder resources between those who had more and those who had less.

This idea connected with feelings of guilt he'd experienced throughout the process. "Any pastor who oversees twelve years of capital stewardship campaigns and spends millions of dollars on a facility should feel some guilt," he says. "I thought, *How can we be spending so much money on this with all the other needs in the world?*"

The need to mark the end of the project, the idea of jubilee, and guilt about having spent so much on themselves led Wevers to an idea: *Let's proclaim a year of jubilee as a church.*

For Calvary, this decision meant they would pause for a year and not raise any money for their own buildings. Instead, they would help build structures in places like South Africa, Haiti, Ecuador, Palestine, Honduras, the Dominican Republic and New York. And they wouldn't just send money: members of the congregation would visit these places. The congregation would celebrate finishing their own home church by sharing their resources with people around the world. The following year they gave away $370,000, and 250 people from their church went on these trips.

When they came back, everything changed. In Wevers's words, they felt "ambushed by God." Their attention shifted from themselves to the world beyond. What they thought would be a brief sabbatical in fact became the new commitment. After these trips people decided they didn't merely want this to be a year of jubilee—they wanted to be a "jubilee church." This journey continues eight years later. As we look at our first practice here, their story is inspiring and instructive about three actions of practicing *attention*: to awaken, to focus and to renew.

Awakening to the Need for Change

We each awaken to justice in different ways. An inspiring young woman I know in Haiti grew up being exploited and abused as a *restavek* (a child living away from her family in domestic servitude). As she got older, she better understood her own situation and decided she wanted to help to prevent other children from suffering like she had. Her attention was awoken in an awful, heartbreaking way that makes me want to cry—and feel deeply proud—every time I think of her experiences as a child, how she talks about the slow healing process and how she shares about Jesus transforming her life so she can now serve the kind of children she once was.

For other people who grew up sheltered from many injustices, awakening may come through friends, a missions trip, a book. It can emerge gradually or come in a Damascus Road-like epiphany.

For Pastor Wevers, after growing up in what he called a "fortress church" (focused only on themselves inside the church walls), he went on a missions trip to Utah as a high schooler with a "red-haired, fiery, evangelistic pastor of a dynamic church." The experience set a path toward ministry that focused its attention outward. Over time this became constrained by the building project, but during the phase-one project Wevers was moved by Shane Claiborne's book *The Irresistible Revolution*, in which Claiborne tells his own story of awakening to faith and justice in college, then going to work with Mother Teresa in Kolkata and then moving to inner-city Philadelphia.

Anger, guilt, sadness, determination, paralysis: one or all of these emotions may surge in us as our attention is drawn to the injustice of the world and to our own desire to make it a little more just. Alicia, in our opening chapter, felt bad as she looked through her mail. Guilt, for example, can wake us up to the need to change. Never feeling guilt is not a state of ecstasy, as Las Vegas advertisements would have us believe, but is actually a sign of numbness unto death.

Wevers was paying attention to this mix of feelings as Calvary Church finished the first phase of their new building and prepared for the next stages, which included market-driven megachurch amenities. They had already put a great deal of energy and money into their own community and were about to spend even more. Wevers knew the situation of the majority peoples in the world. He slowed down enough to pay attention. He knew there were churches and schools that couldn't afford to put up simple structures. Awakening to justice, however it happens, involves listening to other people's lives.

Wings of Desire is a film by the German director Wim Wenders. The story is told from the perspective of an angel who no longer wants to be an angel. The angel isn't rebelling against God; there are tender scenes of him and other angels providing spiritual comfort by being (invisibly) near a feeble old man, a lonely woman, a man injured in a car accident. But this angel wants to experience human time, aching, love, taste and the warm friction of rubbing his hands together. The angels' experience is limited to black and white, not color, to being able to experience the spiritual, not physical. The film reflects on the beautiful vulnerability of being human.

The storytelling technique that makes the movie a profound experience is that the angels (and viewers) can hear people's thoughts. We hear the inner lives of people we normally rush past in busyness. The way this movie and its sequel, *Faraway, So Close*, listen to other people's lives shifted something in me when I first watched them twenty years ago. Art can awaken our attention. The movies made me more awake to the subtle sadness, frustration and joy in people as I stood in line at the bank. In the weeks after seeing the movie, I remember having to fight off tears standing in a grocery store line as I paid attention to the people around me.

One of the Bible's refrains is that we should care for widows and orphans. They're specified both because their needs are greater and because they are pushed to the margins—out of sight, out of mind—sometimes by society's neglect, other times by society's willful choice. Scripture calls us to listen: "Religion that God our Father accepts as pure and faultless is this: to look after orphans and widows in their distress" (Jas 1:27 NIV). The whispers of their lives demand our attention.

We practice awakening to justice by choosing who we talk with, what stories we read, what trips we take, what art we take in. Wevers invited his church to awaken to justice by giving to and traveling around the world. Church members chose to put themselves in situations where their eyes would be opened.

Later in this chapter we'll hear how this changed the life of Laurie Poll, a member at Calvary and the principal of a nearby elementary school. Which also reminds me of how programs like Teach For America place recent college graduates into under-served communities for two years. The experience opens their eyes to educational challenges and also pulls back the curtain on big systemic issues of wealth, poverty, government represen-tation and race that many of them didn't know in-depth before.

Part of this practice of attention involves asking ourselves, What breaks my heart? In the world, my country or my neighborhood, what makes me angry because it should be better? Questions like this can awaken our attention for how we're called to serve the kingdom.

We can also take advice on this practice from Mark Barden, whose first-grade son, Daniel, was murdered in the Sandy Hook Elementary School shootings. "Pick your eyes up from the sidewalk and look at people," he said at the Sojourners Summit.[1] We should pay attention, and we shouldn't let other people feel invisible. We seek to love, and to be strengthened by grace, to be able to do this.

> The problem is that when we start paying attention, we may start to hear voices we hadn't previously heard.

The problem is that when we start paying attention, we may start to hear voices we hadn't previously heard. We realize how deep and wide the problems are. Then we realize that we must focus.

FOCUSING SO WE HELP WELL

Those inner voices and the daily blaring headlines of injustice call us in a thousand worthwhile directions. The moments in *Wings of Desire* when I could hear everyone's inner voices simultaneously, I couldn't understand any of them. To practice attention in a way that serves justice well, we need to deliberately focus so we don't spread our efforts scattershot and make no real difference.

That first year of jubilee at Calvary Church, after 250 people returned from visiting projects they'd supported around the world, led to two decisions. They decided to throw out the glossy brochures they had already printed to promote the next phase of the building plan, and they decided to focus. Rather than committing to a wide range of projects around the globe, they would devote their effort primarily on one country.

They chose Haiti because there were tremendous needs and travel was accessible. They educated the congregation. One year they would give to help build a school so the church would learn about education needs. The next year they would purchase and send a mobile clinic and learned about health issues. By being focused the members of the congregation became more deeply connected to Haiti and its people, and more knowledgeable about the country's situation. They also learned how to do missions and development work more effectively.

Not that everything went smoothly. The first year started badly, says Wevers, because they handed a $60,000 check to a small missions partner in Haiti without *partnering* that included good accountability. (We'll look at partnering under practice four.) They learned. If you don't have focus, it's easy to keep repeating the same mistakes—or not even know you're making them.

I serve on the board of a charitable foundation focused on human trafficking and rights in Southeast Asia and Haiti. By deciding on clear issues and geographical areas, the foundation is able to make informed decisions about the projects it supports. Its staff has become experts in these areas, so they are a source of knowledge and connections in addition to money. Focusing means having a yes that helps us say no to many other worthwhile, heartbreaking needs.

A Haitian proverb says, *Pise gaye pa fe kim* (When your stream of pee hits the ground too widely, it doesn't make foam). It's an earthy way to say if our attention is too scattered, we won't make much difference.

Physiologically, the brain stem is the more primal part of the brain that responds to hunger and danger. It's the part of the brain that makes us jump out of a car's path without having to think; we just react. The prefrontal cortex is the thoughtful, deliberate manager of the brain stem and other lobes. The brain stem and prefrontal cortex communicate, but compete over which gets to direct our attention.

In the work of justice, there are important moments to react, metaphorically speaking, with the lower parts of the brain that are attuned to survival, like giving to direct relief work after a devastating tsunami, when food, water and rescue is needed immediately.

But most of the time we do best to let our prefrontal cortex discern between our gut reaction, emotions and best analysis so that we're asking: How can we focus our attention to effectively help this slow kingdom to come?

Calvary Church keeps its focus by engaging hearts and minds, and by keeping their message fresh. The congregation reads a book together annually. Every Christmas church members give more than $100,000 to a specific missions project in Haiti, knowing they will hear frequent progress reports. (They have helped build a school and training center with the organization I codirect.) Calvary's missions pastor has been to Haiti about thirty times in the past seven years. They facilitate exchange, such as bringing to their church a children's choir from the community where Calvary helped build a school. The choir sang and got the whole church dancing with them. By honing their focus, the congregation is able to direct its attention in such a way that they see the right needs, follow through with available resources, grow in expertise and develop relationships.

> We're accountable for the responsibilities we're trusted with, not for all the needs around us.

Jesus told a parable about several people receiving money (talents) to manage individually (Mt 25:14-30). One of the lessons is that we're each responsible for the gifts God entrusts to us. It's important and freeing to discern a clear calling. Part of how we can do this is by reading Scripture in ways that help us listen more deeply to God, ourselves and others. We can take fasts from media that distract our ability to focus our attention. There are ways to organize meetings (like one method called Open Space[2]) that can serve community development by helping us focus on people's most important needs.

We're accountable for the responsibilities we're trusted with, not for all the needs around us.

Renewing Our Commitment

After we awaken to justice and discern our focus, we get to ride that wave of energy until we're carried by a comfy chariot into the kingdom in heaven, right? Probably not. Most of us will lag in our concentration. We'll drift from our mission or doubt it entirely. We'll feel discouraged and guilty because we can't respond to all the needs around us. Our vision will blur. We will need renewal. I've watched this happen to myself and others.

Sustaining attention in the work of justice can be difficult, which is why the leaders at Calvary have worked hard to help their congregation do it. This is a marathon. They report regularly on their projects; seeing progress can encourage everyone. Relationships are another way people are continually renewed, so they nurture connections. More than eight hundred people from the church have gone on missions trips in the past eight years. Many church members forgo traditional vacations so they can participate in these trips. As people share their experiences, it creates a common bond in the congregation. Hearts are renewed through relationships with people, a country and issues that keep everything meaningful and dynamic.

Several times a year I visit the Haitian family my wife and I lived with for seven months when we first moved there thirteen years ago. If I didn't spend time with them four or five times a year, I don't think I'd still be working there. In my first book I wrote about navigating the many differences between us. Now when I'm with them, it feels something like home. When I'm sitting in their yard, as moonlight comes through the palm branches, talking with the seventeen-year-old young man who used to sit on my wife's lap as a four-year-old, I'm renewed. When the couple shares their concerns and joys, and I do likewise, I'm renewed. A few years ago was their grandmother's funeral; amidst the loud wailing, even in the heartbreak, I'm renewed by gratitude for having been able to know a woman as beautiful, dignified and playful as she was. Visiting our god-daughter at her nearby school, which our organization helped rebuild after the earthquake, I'm renewed. Through sharing experiences of joy and laughter as well as the challenges of working through uncomfortable expectations, my attention to the work of justice is renewed.

Sometimes church missions trips are profound for those who travel, but the effect doesn't ripple out far beyond the team. Calvary's ministry focus and its emphasis on engaging so many people in the church have meant the congregation is on a journey together—literally and metaphorically. Members understand why there is still no cappuccino bar in the lobby and there are a few leaks in the roof.

If you're an American involved in work outside of the United States, inevitably someone at home will ask, "Why are you going to help in _____ when there are so many problems right here?" The most charitable interpretation of this question is that the person is concerned about attention spreading too thin. But Wevers thinks the focus on Haiti actually strengthens and renews the church's overall mission, which means they engage better locally as well as helping keep the smaller internal church quibbles in appropriate perspective. They are renewed in their ministry through the relationship with Haiti and the energy and perspective they gain.

"It's almost impossible," says Wevers, "to become a jubilee church that is globally involved without people coming back and saying, 'You know, I can't go to Haiti three or four times a year, but I want to be engaged in the world and find needs and address them right here in Holland, Michigan.' Global engagement has fueled people to come back and say, 'I can open up my home for emergency issues with foster care' or 'I can take in an international student' or 'I can volunteer in recovery ministry or jail ministry.' To me, a church's global ministry is secondary to local. Our global jubilee giving and working has fueled local ministry, which has been a sweet ripple-down effect."

Laurie Poll's life reflects this. "This jubilee thing has really messed up our lives," Laurie laughs as she tells me about being part of this transformation at Calvary Church. "But in a good way! I'm so grateful for the power of this invitation to shift my attention."

Laurie, an elementary school principal, has attended Calvary Church for about twenty-five years. She's married and has two sons, ages eighteen and twenty-one. I've had the chance to meet her, and it doesn't take long to feel her positive energy.

When Calvary took its first Jubilee trips, she went to Queens, New York, and painted a fence for a week, which she found irritating. "I know that makes me sound like a terrible person," she says, but she thought she could make a more relevant contribution.

The next year a group was going to Haiti to help with education. That seemed like a better fit. The first few visits were good, but then something clicked on the next few trips. She's now part of an annual teacher training for seven Haitian schools, an experience that she says has changed her life, her family's life and her school in Michigan.

"We started to understand, after several experiences, how we could really serve and help the teachers," she says now after eight trips. "Then the fact that we kept going back meant we kept improving. The connection deepened. All year long we're meeting and having conversations at home about how we can do the next training even better. I've also seen how the Haitian teachers have grown in trusting us because we come back and prepare and work hard."

What changes has the awakening and focus of her attention made back home?

"We haven't sold our home in Michigan yet, but we wrestle with this kind of question. My husband and sons tease me about still getting my nails done. I joke that Jesus still loves me enough that he doesn't mind if I look cute sometimes. But more seriously, we've given away a lot of money to serve Haiti. It's become a huge, wonderful part of our lives. And this jubilee experience has shifted our family's attention toward what is important in our home too. I think this has happened at the school where I'm principal as well. In the month of July, for our family or for the teachers who are part of the training, it would be great to go to the beach, but we're going to go down to work hard and sweat in Haiti."

She says she grew up in a family that wanted to serve. But through the experience of going to Queens and then Haiti her attention keeps getting awakened and focused, more each time. Then she and her husband wanted their boys to have a similar awakening. "All along the way," she says, "the invitations from Calvary were so important in making this possible."

Pastor Wevers paid attention. Calvary Church paid attention, and this included inviting people like Laurie to pay attention in new ways, which she did. They help each other to awaken, focus and renew.

"Jubilee invites all of us to find our place," she says. "Some people are helping in local ministries, some are going to Haiti, others help by doing dishes after our church dinner. We're able to honor everyone's talents and what they feel led to do with a common vision for the whole church."

Whether for a large church or small, or for a person like Laurie or you or me, if our work in justice is awakened and focused, we're led on a journey during which, if we practice attention, we can find continuous renewal.

The Spiritual Benefits of Attention

Simone Weil, a French philosopher, theologian and activist around the time of World War II, wrote a remarkable essay in which she connects the discipline of schoolwork with that of prayer.[3] She argues the main benefit of working hard at school is to develop our attention, which in turn helps us improve at praying.

Similarly, attention to justice should lead to the deepening of our spiritual lives because as we practice attention in our approach to justice we also

> **Attention to justice should lead to the deepening of our spiritual lives.**

more attentively pray for guidance in working for God's kingdom to come on earth as in heaven. We need to wait on God, which is a tough balance to strike as we also need to push urgently to break down barriers of injustice.

Weil's attention was so developed, in both academic work and in prayer, that she would sometimes have mystical experiences when she put her full attention to reciting the Lord's Prayer. It's only a slight exaggeration to say a more common problem for most of us is making it through the Lord's Prayer without our thoughts wandering before we get to "amen." Fortunately, in addition to schoolwork we have many tools that can help us strengthen our practice of attention, such as reading Scripture in ways that help us listen more deeply and with others, or taking fasts from media that can distract our concentration.

While writing this chapter I spent four days of retreat at a Benedictine monastery, pausing throughout the day for silence, prayer and chanting Scripture. Lunches with the monks were in silence, but we talked during dinner. I explained what I was working on, and the monks around the table shared how the reflective rhythm of their lives enables them to focus on what is most important. I try to incorporate bits of their wisdom into the slightly more chaotic rhythm of a life with two young kids and both parents working outside the home.

Retreats as individuals, families, churches and organizations can help us renew our attention. Scientific studies have said that our brains can pay better attention if even three times a day we slow down to meditate for five minutes. Spiritual disciplines like those articulated by Richard Foster in his book *Celebration of Discipline* can be understood as disciplines for the *cultivation of attention.*

This practice will look different for each of us, but is vital for all of us. And it can be as simple as setting down this book and for five minutes sitting with God and pondering the question, "What breaks my heart?" If that sounds too hard, you can start with two minutes.

Attention, Weil says, is what makes up our love for God and our neighbor, which is why this practice needs awakening, focus and renewal.[4] Calvary Church shows that this kind of attention can lead to jubilee.

CONFESSION

The Posture for Engaging

*The Lord is not slow about his promise, as some think
of slowness, but is patient with you, not wanting
any to perish, but all to come to repentance.*

2 PETER 3:9

*Above all, don't lie to yourself. The man who lies to
himself . . . cannot distinguish the truth within him, or
around him, and so loses all respect for himself and
for others. And having no respect he ceases to love.*

FYODOR DOSTOYEVSKY, *THE BROTHERS KARAMAZOV*

One Sunday morning a few years ago, the church sanctuary
was empty except for a few of us talking near the exit. My
son, two at the time, was running between the pews, not yet tall
enough to see over them, like he was adventuring through a
medieval maze of ten-foot-high hedges.

These pews have built-in kneelers, padded benches that fold
down to about six inches off the floor. Early in the service when
the congregation confesses sins together, we fold them down

to kneel for prayer. As he dashed between pews, my main concern was that he'd find a pencil, wield it as a sword and then trip and impale his eye. Instead, he stopped to pull down one of the kneelers, which dropped hard (fortunately his toes weren't crushed). Then he paused and knelt like he's seen us do in the service.

He got up, went to the next pew, pulled down the kneeler and knelt briefly. Then he went to the next. There are two or three kneelers per pew. He pulled down one after another, regularly stopping to kneel, then moving to the next. He was consumed by the task with all the concentration of a master craftsman. Eventually he pulled down enough kneelers for 125 people, half the church.

In the service an hour earlier, as a church we had said aloud, "We confess that we are captive to sin and cannot free ourselves. . . . We have not loved you with our whole heart; we have not loved our neighbors as ourselves."

I didn't grow up in churches that had kneelers, but for the past nine years in this church I've been grateful for the weekly chance to confess at the beginning of worship. (When I make it to church on time, my wife would add—okay, there's personal confession number one.) Over the past twenty years I've also learned that kneeling for confession is the right posture for entering into the work of justice—with humility, supplication and vulnerability. If we don't lower ourselves before God and neighbors, we will fail at lasting change; we need to be transformed ourselves as we work for the world to become more just. The work of justice is interwoven with the need for healing, and anyone who wants to work for healing is invited to make confession a regular practice: "Therefore confess your sins to one another, and pray for one another, so that you may be healed" (Jas 5:16).

What tender hope we're invited into through this promise. When we practice confession in our work for justice, we find freedom to work for the healing of others at the same time we are healed.

After college I was going to move to Europe to work with a refugee ministry. The missions agency first required us to spend four months training at their Chicago home office. During this time most other trainees spent time learning languages like Tagalog and German. I was going to live near London and decided not to work on an English accent, so I had extra time. In the small basement library I discovered the journals of the nineteenth-century Danish philosopher-theologian Søren Kierkegaard. I'm not sure I'd heard of him before. I had taken a few religion courses in college, but had majored in business and minored in political science. (My Christian college was generally more into Ronald Reagan's free market than Søren Kierkegaard's existential dilemmas.)

During those four months, I lost and found myself repeatedly in his journals. The intensity of Kierkegaard's inner search has nourished my justice work ever since. He said that life can only be understood backward, but it must be lived forward.[1] We slow down to look backward for self-examination and understanding so we can then better move forward. No, we won't ever move forward with perfect understanding. But when this backward-forward movement includes confession, it can become a cycle of healing that frees us to see more clearly how to become agents of healing and justice.

The Gospel of Mark tells the story of Jesus arriving in Bethsaida, where people brought a blind man and asked Jesus to heal him.

He took the blind man by the hand and led him out of the village; and when he had put saliva on his eyes and laid his hands on him, he asked him, "Can you see anything?" And the man looked up and said, "I can see people, but they look like trees, walking." Then Jesus laid his hands on his eyes again; and he looked intently and his sight was restored, and he saw everything clearly. (Mk 8:23-25)

Jesus led him step by step. The blind man followed step by step. The healing didn't happen in a flash. Then Jesus touched the man and put spit on his eyes. It helped, but things were still blurry. People looked like trees. After doing it again, then the man could see clearly.

I love this story of *gradual healing* because it affirms how gradual the process often is to be healed and to help others to heal. Sin can blind us—so we are unaware of selfishness that leads us to exploit when we intend to help. Sin can blind us—so our hurts guide us instead of other people's hopes. Sin can blind us—so we can't see the needs under the surface.

We confess our temptations and vulnerabilities so we can be healed gradually, like the man in Bethsaida, both for what we have done and what we have left undone. Healing helps us to see so we can keep following, step by step, toward helping each other to flourish. As we see, we can be guided not by shame that blinds us but instead by a clearer vision of God's kingdom.

The following eight confessions might feel a little uncomfortable at times, but they are worth it if we then become better at love. Right? Practicing *confession* can help us keep moving forward step by step.

CONFESS YOUR MIXED MOTIVES

In U2's song "One," Bono sings, "Have you come here to play Jesus / To the lepers in your head?"[2] Yes, if you are involved in justice work, you probably have. So have I. This isn't bad. Just honest. We can find freedom confessing that our own need for healing is part of why we work for the healing of justice.

We come to the work of justice not as purely altruistic people, but, as Luther said, we are *simul justus et peccator*, simultaneously saints and sinners. I've always found it important to be upfront about this with myself and with others. We want to help lepers, but we also seek to heal the lepers in our own heads. Confessing like this can disarm the power of my desire for success, or my ego, or my search for meaning, or the way pain from my past motivates me. For example, I'm freed to practice respect (which we'll discuss more in chapter four) with other people and avoid using them as tools in my own search for meaning or success.

It can be hard to admit mixed motives because a nice part about working for justice is escaping our own selfishness. In the first chapter, we heard about Yanique's struggle with moving from radical ideals to cynicism, which included realizing her mixed motives. Confession will help free her to move through cynicism to a more mature, durable hope. While circling over Port-au-Prince, preparing to land six days after the catastrophic earthquake in 2010, I found myself writing, "Like angels, we help. Like vultures, we scavenge on the suffering of others to feed our hunger for meaning.

> **When we enter someone's life to help, we also have the potential to hurt.**

Purity cannot be checked in or carried on for these flights. The baggage is ourselves. Always ourselves."[3] Even responding to tragedy, I wasn't made pure.

This is good to admit because when we enter someone's life to help, we also have the potential to hurt. We owe it to people we serve to be aware of how our motivations influence us. We confess them so we can continue to be transformed to best serve God's kingdom.

While living in Haiti I kept needing to examine my conflicted motivations. From a North American view, what I was doing looked self-sacrificial—without electricity, running water or many comforts. But how much of it was for me, and how was that infecting my work? Confessing this along the way (especially through writing in a journal late at night by the light of a kerosene lamp) opened the way for deeper relationships and serving in a complex place in need of justice.

I've found healing when I honestly confess the many conflicting voices I hear so that I'm freed to follow the call of my vocation, which the novelist Fredrick Buechner put so well: "The place God calls you to is the place where your deep gladness and the world's deep hunger meet."[4]

God and neighbor, I confess my mixed motives. Help the fruit of my efforts to be beautiful and just.

CONFESS THE DESIRE TO FEEL GOOD WHEN YOU HELP

We confess our impulse to help in ways that feel immediately good to us, so we can be freed to fully engage both our hearts *and* minds for more lasting work.

A few weeks after the Haiti earthquake I was walking through an airport hanger in Florida that was a drop-off center for the generous donations pouring in. Pallets stacked with supplies stretched in every direction, and volunteers busily prepared life's staples—food, water, shelter, medicine—to be transported to people whose lives had collapsed in forty-five seconds. People in the organization, some of whom I knew, were working hard on little sleep.

As I walked through the hanger past one stack of boxes, I heard a staff member, who was orienting a dozen new volunteers, say in a tired monotone, "Over there is a pallet full of cases of donated barbecue sauce." He then added, saying what he probably would have kept to himself under less sleep-deprived conditions, "Haitians are dying. They do not need barbecue sauce."

One hopes the barbecue sauce wasn't a cynical corporate tax write-off. But even if donated with the best intentions, it's a reminder that helping well takes our hearts *and* our heads.

It's not bad to want to feel good when we seek to help generously. So what freedom can we find by confessing this? We can ask whether we're giving things needed by the homeless shelter or what is most rewarding or convenient for us to give. When I confess (that is, honestly reveal) my desire to help in a way that makes me feel good, I'm freed to be guided by an even deeper desire. Instead of *What giving will make me feel best?* I can be freed into the better question *What giving is the best way to help others?*

We should still experience the joy of loving generously, but through the practice of confession we're also freed to ask the right questions, consult experts and follow good approaches.

God and neighbor, I confess that I'm tempted to contribute in ways that make me feel best, not that help most. Help me to slow down to serve my neighbor in the best way possible.

CONFESS YOUR PUBLIC GESTURES

We confess we sometimes overvalue public gestures for justice so we can be freed to invest in substantial things that aren't immediately visible.

TOMS shoes (worn by Yanique) pioneered a "buy one, give one" model of social entrepreneurship. For each pair of shoes purchased, the company would provide a pair of shoes for someone poor. The beauty of the approach was its direct simplicity. But this for-profit-and-for-social-good model was initially much better at marketing *symbols of justice* than at doing the *work of justice*, which a number of development experts criticized. TOMS has improved this and shown a desire to understand its impact.[5] But fast success revealed how we're vulnerable to buying the message without knowing the substance behind it.

Shopping ethically is important, and I'm not questioning the motives of anyone who has bought the shoes, including many friends who are good people who like to help. But it's no secret that marketing geniuses try to exploit all our desires, including our desire to do good. They can tap into our desire to help others while also using our vulnerability of wanting to be seen as compassionate, justice-minded people by the brands we wear. So, we need to ask whether what we're doing is making a real difference below the marketing surface. Am I clicking a new cause because I want to be seen a certain way?

We need to take public stands, but public, symbolic gestures will tempt us to shortcuts in how we make decisions and try to motivate people. This isn't a new problem. Jesus addressed this temptation as related to piety and justice in his mountainside sermon:

> Beware of practicing your piety before others in order to be seen by them; for then you have no reward from your Father in heaven.
>
> So whenever you give alms, do not sound a trumpet before you, as the hypocrites do in the synagogues and in the streets, so that they may be praised by others. . . . But when you give alms, do not let your left hand know what your right hand is doing, so that your alms may be done in secret; and your Father who sees in secret will reward you. (Mt 6:1-4)

Jesus' guidance isn't easy today when social media means we can invite others along the path of justice while also proclaiming from atop Mount Zuckerberg how good and adventurous we are.

(I offer a second personal confession: I've written books and articles about my adventures in justice.)

When we confess this and follow practices that help us mature together, we are freed to help more substantially. On our knees, we see all this more clearly through eyes that are healed.

God and neighbor, I confess I want to be seen *as good. Free me* to do *what is good.*

CONFESS YOUR HERO COMPLEX

We confess that sometimes we make ourselves seem like saviors, so that we can be freed to tell a truer story. This is related to our confessions about mixed motives and public gestures, yet distinct enough we should be aware.

In *Spiritual Theology*, my former professor Diogenes Allen wrote, "With vainglory, we crave notice of our achievements [like the symbolic gestures discussed earlier]; with pride, we take full credit for the progress we have made and do not think that God has been involved at all, let alone been our indispensible helper."[6]

In the context of justice, I think what Christians need to confess about their pride isn't so much about taking credit away from God but from the people we help. One version of this is sometimes referred to as White Man's Burden, which takes its name from a Rudyard Kipling poem that describes how it would be noble for colonialists to exploit people under the guise of helping them.

Practicing confession is one way to guard against paternalism in both extreme and more subtle ways.

For example, we can tell stories of justice in a way that discounts other people's *agency*—that is, their ability to act and choose to shape their own lives and futures. Invisible Children's "Kony 2012" campaign made Joseph Kony infamous as a way to raise awareness and increase pressure to stop this evil warlord in central Africa who maimed many and made children into killers. The video seems to have contributed to pressure to contain him, which is fantastic, but for the sake of our confession it's worth noting that a number of commentators from Uganda and other countries strongly criticized how this version cast the hero of the story—namely, Americans. It could have better respected the story of people they were trying to help. People in Uganda and other nearby countries had suffered most. They had lost children. They had done the most work to try to stop Kony. They had done the most to help the children suffering in his wake.

This confession invites us to consider how casting ourselves as heroes of justice may cut short the credit other people deserve for their agency. Because I've also been guilty at times in my writing, fundraising and trying to motivate people, I'm aware of this temptation. It can happen when we walk into a church meeting and think of ourselves as the expert without making the effort to listen well to others. It can happen when we see people struggling, and judge that they should just pull themselves up by their bootstraps even though we don't know all their circumstances. It can happen when we assume certain people don't have as much God-given potential as we do and are just charity cases for us to take mercy on.

> Confession helps free us to humbly lift up the agency of others and be wary of being the hero of our own stories.

We should be aware of how we tell the stories of justice. We should be aware of the capacity and contributions of people around us. Confession helps free us to humbly lift up the agency of others and be wary of being the hero of our own stories. We can find freedom from pride tempting us to inflate our own importance and leading us into bad attempts at helping. Confession frees us to respect each other's stories and to partner for the thriving of others.

God and neighbor, I confess that I claim too much credit. Grow my humility and show me how to rightly give credit to others.

CONFESS YOUR COMPASSION FATIGUE

After working in Haiti for more than a dozen years, I can't count the number of times I've been asked, "Will Haiti ever get better?" There are problematic assumptions behind this question, as though we could judge others and dismiss hope like that. But I want to focus on the positive: It's good for us to confess honestly that our compassion can get exhausted, whether with a needy friend always in crisis or when hearing about a country like Haiti, where many encouraging things are happening but the headlines and appeals are often heartbreaking and the macroprogress is slow.

Like Alicia in the opening chapter, sometimes we read a charity fundraising letter and wonder why it's my responsibility whether people are sick or healthy, saved or lost. It can all feel too heavy to carry.

We shouldn't feel guilty about confessing our fatigue. We work for justice at our church or office or home as though the results are up to us, so at times we can burn out. I don't know anyone who doesn't get exhausted and frustrated along the way of the slow kingdom coming, whatever your vocation.

We should confess compassion fatigue so that we stay honest and sensitive to how this affects us and the people we're helping. We confess our fatigue so we're reminded of the importance of regular sabbath rest. We confess our fatigue because sometimes we need our community to carry us when the vision gets blurry. Sometimes we'll help carry others.

We also confess so we can be renewed by love. All the confessions in this chapter are ways to seek freedom. Practicing confession prepares us to experience many mini-resurrections into hope, through which God frees us into faithfulness. If you're at all like me, you'll end up needing to be resurrected all the time.

God and neighbor, I confess I'm sometimes empty of compassion. Renew me in the deep gladness of the call to work for justice.

CONFESS YOUR PRIVILEGE

We confess that injustice weaves through power, race, sexuality, gender, nationality. In this confession each of us who somehow benefits can seek the freedom to take responsibility to participate in change.

I'm in Haiti regularly; my vocation is justice work. In the past I've lived quite radically, but right now my life looks very much like that of a white, straight, married, educated, middle-class American man. This doesn't mean life is easy, but it *does mean* it's much easier for me than for a lot of other people. At my worst, when I'm giving in to shortcut temptations, I need to write a confession like this for myself:

Confession of My Privilege
to Mostly Accept the Way Things Are

I, the undersigned, do hereby admit that I spend most of my days

- overwhelmingly doing what's best for me and my family instead of really seeing everyone as sister and brother;
- mildly protesting against injustice systems (e.g., voting, giving donations, providing some succor to victims of

drought or discrimination but doing nothing to fundamentally change the order of things); and

- allowing the American government to repeatedly act in its own (that is, our) self-interest to the disadvantage of people who are poorest and weakest.

I, the undersigned, do admit that the resulting benefits are

- my opportunity to live with relative physical and caloric safety;

- my continued relative financial prosperity though it is rooted partly in the murder of Native Americans, blood of African slaves, current unfair agricultural policies and trade deals with other countries, continued discriminatory practices and other ugly things; and

- my passport will let me come and go where I please, even as the passports of others will keep them out of here so it doesn't ruin the good thing we have going.

And I, the undersigned, confess that the costs are

- that I have to live either ignoring part of reality or with a partially anesthetized heart; and

- that others have to live on faith, but with little chance.

Signed: *Kent Annan*   Date: *today*

Something like this may well not apply to you, but if to some extent it does, then it's important to get into an honest and humble posture (like on the kneelers my son pulled down) as we enter the work of justice.

Ta-Nehisi Coates wrote a powerful cover story for *The Atlantic* magazine in June 2014. The title was "The Case for Reparations." The subtitle: "250 Years of Slavery. 90 Years of Jim

Crow. 60 Years of Separate but Equal. 35 Years of State-Sanctioned Redlining. Until we Reckon With the Compounding Moral Debts of Our Ancestors, America Will Never Be Whole."

The fifteen thousand–word essay is a moving call to recognize the abuse of privilege and need for societal confession—not just saying sorry but taking that confession posture so we can then get to the work of thinking through and practicing justice in response. Coates makes a compelling case for this as the only path to a hopeful future. Three months after the essay was published, this pain surfaced nationally after a young African American man was shot six times by a police officer in Ferguson, Missouri. The subsequent tension between the town's mostly black population and mostly white police and politicians (whose abuse of power and lack of listening ratcheted up the tension and was later called out by the US Department of Justice) became yet another example illustrating Coates's points. In following months, case after similar heart-rending case came to light.

One of the thoughts I had while reading the essay was about the 1.5 million Americans who may spend over $2 billion to go on short-term missions trips every year.[7] Maybe before a small group is sent from a church to address injustice in another country—like building a church or working in a school—the whole congregation should go through a public confession about the way our own country has, for example, exploited Native Americans and African Americans, and how that pain and exploitation still creates ripples today. Or maybe the congregation should confess what is happening right now with race and economics in its own community. These confessions may come when a church's attention first awakes to injustice, or it could happen after they come back from trips like Calvary Church took and then see their own neighborhood with new eyes. Some congregations have practiced confession this way, but many may be missing out on the freedom and responsibility this could lead to in its ministry.

Jesus said, "Why do you see the speck in your neighbor's eye, but do not notice the log in your own eye? Or how can you say to your neighbor, 'Let me take the speck out of your eye,' while the log is in your own eye?" (Mt 7:3-4). Before we go to help others, should we confess the dynamics of privilege in our own backyard? For Jesus, confession includes recognizing a problem and also acting to rectify it, "You hypocrite, first take the log out of your own eye, and then you will see clearly to take the speck out of your neighbor's eye" (Mt 7:5).

Seeking this freedom collectively is important, as is the need to personally practice confession so I can better see whether there is a log in my own eye that needs removing. Can we solve injustice problems *out there* while unaware that we're benefitting from the privilege of unjust history and policies *right here*? I truly believe and have seen how practicing confession allows us to experience deeper joy while working for justice.

We confess so we can make new decisions and renew commitments. We do it, like Jesus says, so our eyes are healed to see our neighbor more clearly

> **Practicing confession allows us to experience deeper joy while working for justice.**

(they're not just blurry trees!). By learning history and reading articles like "The Case for Reparations," we pray about and meditate on important and needed changes that we can influence (practicing *attention*). We're freed to learn through deeper friendships and partnerships and being vulnerable. For example, if you're part of the dominant cultural group, find respectful ways to engage with the minority where you live. We listen and learn to become allies. We resist temptations to be confession masochists, because for some this kind of guilt can feed tendencies of self-denigration or self-importance and not lead to other active practices of justice. The litmus test of good confession is whether it leads to removing the log, to healing, to vision and then to changed action. The only way to true hope is the way of truth. Confession paves our way.

God and neighbor, I confess the privileges that benefit me. Help me to give them away again and again.

CONFESS YOUR PAIN CAUSED AND RECEIVED

We confess that we have caused or received pain. This is part of living in a kingdom that is not yet fully come. This pain can be inflicted at a national level; we can also feel or cause this pain personally with someone else. Pain is a result of injustices past, and they can be roadblocks toward future justice. Confession, though, can help clear the way.

Every three years InterVarsity Christian Fellowship and its sister organizations host the Urbana Student Missions Conference, which I've had the chance to attend several times. In 2006 the Japanese and Korean international students gathered for a joint worship time. After prayer and singing, a Japanese student spontaneously stood in front of the group and apologized for the Japanese occupation of Korea from 1910 to 1945, which happened long before any of them were born. A tension under the surface was confessed. Tears started to flow. Koreans then stood and apologized for the hatred they had collectively felt through the generations toward Japan and its people. This led to more prayer and worship that was so much deeper and more joyful, more kingdom-like than was possible before practicing confession.

The beautiful example of these groups point us toward corporate and individual opportunities to be honest about how our past can hold us back from a more kingdom future. We're pointed in the direction of healing.

God and neighbor, I confess that I have caused pain of, and am hurt by, injustice. Help me to participate in healing for others and myself.

CONFESS YOUR LONGING FOR CHANGE

We just examined seven confessions of vulnerability, and now we will end with a positive confession. We confess the hope of life, now and forever, that God's love is stronger than death and will make all things right—and that by grace we participate right now in *making things right*. It's the hope, in the words of Martin Luther King Jr., that the "arc of the moral universe is long but it bends toward justice."[8]

The psalms and the prophets echo with the desire of justice for ourselves and others—for a different world than the one we have. This isn't confessing temptation or weakness, but it's another important form of confession. At times I bottle up my longing for change. This aching sadness and hope makes me want to weep in a way that scares me because I might not be able to stop. Saying this doesn't feel melodramatic. If there isn't one already, there should be a mythological figure who weeps continuously on our behalf.

Maybe hidden on the banks where the Tigris and Euphrates Rivers meet stands a giant, mysterious, living, breathing willow tree—some kind of a mystical tree and an angel. From each of the drooping branches and leaves teardrops fall day and night. Maybe this is what became of the Tree of the Knowledge of Good and Evil. It became this weeping willow that, once its fruit was plucked, has been weeping ever since with that knowledge of good and evil, of joy and suffering, all day and night. It weeps with longing.

Ultimately, in the midst of all the confessions in this chapter about the darkness and light in us and around us, we most strongly confess our hope that the "Lord is not slow about his promise, as some think of slowness, but is patient with you, not wanting any to perish, but all to come to repentance" (2 Pet 3:9). Paul confesses his motives and actions are a mixed mess, "For I do not do what I want, but I do the very thing I hate" (Rom 7:15), but then confesses his longing for change, "We know that the whole creation has been groaning in labor pains until now" (Rom 8:22).

Yes, our practice of confessing our vulnerabilities should always include the hope that "the one who began a good work among you will bring it to completion by the day of Jesus Christ" (Phil 1:6). We hope for forgiveness and protection but also for much more. We seek to become active testimony to that good work among us, step by step.

Confession is heavy. Confession is light.

Confession produces freedom and restores right relationships, which releases the river of God's justice to roll down. Yes, that river is sometimes fed by streams of tears. Confession includes lament, which is a kind of longing for the wrong to be made right, even if it's too late. We need mourning to be able to continue with honesty and with full hearts. For almost twenty years my friend Luke and I have had an ongoing conversation about lament's role in justice. He wrote a book titled *Spirit Speech: Lament and Celebration in Preaching,* and my second book is largely about lament. Now he is dean of the Duke University Chapel and is the first African American to hold this position. He traveled with me to Haiti after

> **Confession produces freedom and restores right relationships, which releases the river of God's justice to roll down.**

the earthquake and taught and led Haitian seminary students in a powerful time of lament. He shared with them how lament, which I think of as a kind of confession, is often a necessary part of hope and justice.

The Sunday morning after a white man, motivated by racial hatred, entered a historic black church in Charleston, South Carolina, and murdered nine people, Leroy Barber, a black ministry leader, and Rick McKinley, a white pastor, created and made available a call to worship that was used by hundreds of churches around the country and included:

> We declare together, oh Lord
> With hearts breaking, eyes weeping and souls stirring
> We will continue to stand and cry and weep with our brothers and sisters
> We will continue to make a place of peace for even the enemies at our table
> We will continue to open our doors and our hearts to those who enter them
> We will continue to seek to forgive as we have been forgiven
> We will continue to love in Jesus' name because you taught us that love conquers all.[9]

When we pay attention to the world, we don't confess with the innocence of a child, like my son when he was pulling down the pew kneelers. But we practice confession like my church had earlier that morning. We knelt and confessed, aware of so many reasons to confess, wanting to be freed. We paused for silent prayer. Then out of the silence we heard the pastor say, "By grace you have been saved. In the name of Jesus Christ, your sins are forgiven."

On Sunday mornings we hear words of hope and lament, longing and healing that keep opening our eyes like the blind man in Bethsaida, and we see the world a little more as God sees it, with God's longing for justice. We then keep living into the freedom for which we have been set free and into the other practices in this book. We should practice confession both individually and collectively. Our confession should address how we have hurt our community; our forgiveness should free us to see more clearly how to love each other. Our longing is that all of creation will be transformed and that our own lives will be too. Sometimes it's not clear if we're confessing to the divine, to others, to ourselves or if it's simply an attempt to say what is true—and that's okay.

God and neighbor, I confess my hope is in you and in this kingdom coming.

RESPECT
The Golden Rule for Helping

Love one another with mutual affection;
outdo one another in showing honor.

ROMANS 12:10

Respect, I think, always implies imagination—
the ability to see one another, across
our inevitable differences, as living souls.

WENDELL BERRY, *THE ART OF THE COMMONPLACE*

You walk down a dirt path in a Haitian village and come to the edge of someone's yard, called a *lakou*. It's more than a yard. Much of life happens outside—washing clothes, repairing farm tools, cooking, eating. Walking directly into this space would be like barging through someone's front door in Pittsburgh. But there's no doorbell to ring or fence to knock on. So you stop at the *lakou*'s edge: a pause along the way of the slow kingdom coming.

You call out, *Honè*, meaning "honor." Saying this announces that you come to visit with honor for them, their family, their property. You're acknowledging their humanity, their dignity, their right of response. You're confirming that it's up to them whether you enter or not, and on what terms. You stand and wait. Will someone respond? Do they want you to come in? Will they accept you and what you bring?

Respè, meaning "respect," is the word you wait to hear, if you're invited in. It may come from someone squatting beside a plastic tub washing clothes, or from someone walking up with a smile to greet you. Perhaps the woman over a pot of rice in the cooking shack recognizes your voice and calls out without seeing you. Or maybe it's someone you've never visited before, and the person you're coming to see walks up without saying *respè* to inquire about the reason for your visit. *Respè* may come if the honor is there. Honor and respect are established as integral to your interactions moving forward.

The ritual of *honè–respè* physically slows one down at the threshold to recognize there is a *you* and an *I*. It slows one down to commit to the work of respect that is ahead. These words are not only said the first time one visits. Best friends who have been visiting each other for forty years still call out *honè* and await *respè*.

Respect is having a due regard for the feelings, wishes and rights of others. *Due regard* outlines the relationship well; that we're each created in God's image fills in the colors. If the person we're visiting or working with bears the very image of our loving Creator, then the regard we owe her is high indeed.

The practice of respect has to happen at every stage of doing justice, loving mercy and walking humbly in the world. If we rush through without slowing down, we may barge past doorways between us and our potential host who we don't realize is there. We may not be offering respect, even if the goal is helping. Sometimes we call out *honè* and need to wait years to build trust before hearing *respè*. The pause honors the different circumstances and concerns, the varying hopes and histories and values, whether we're relating to a next-door neighbor or a community on the other side of the world. If justice work involves helping people find their way into more respectful circumstances, then every step must be taken while practicing respect. The end and means must be the same.

"In everything do to others as you would have them do to you," Jesus said (Mt 7:12). We're often inspired by this Golden Rule to help others, but the inspiration stays only so deep. People are walking barefoot where the terrain is tough and shoelessness can make someone uncomfortable and vulnerable to disease. It's good to think, *If I didn't have shoes in that situation, I'd want shoes. Let's give them shoes!*

The question is whether the Golden Rule will slow us down enough to show respect by considering every implication. That is, will we take the more rigorous (and more loving) path of applying the Golden Rule systemically with a long-term view rather than individually with more immediate compassion payoff. We may think giving away shoes is the answer. But will the local shoe vendors be put out of business if the market is flooded with free shoes? What if the donated shoes wear down too quickly and cause other health problems? Who will gain or lose power in the local community because of how the channel is set up to distribute the free shoes? Does it contribute to any other systemic problems if the shoes come from white Westerners who give them for free? Would there be a more cost-effective way to help people to buy their own shoes? We take time to ask important questions and learn from the answers (which we'll look at more closely in the upcoming practice of *truthing*).[1]

> **Practicing respect through listening, imagining and promoting rights can guide us toward the slow kingdom coming.**

Honè-respè slows down to see things in their true complexity and then emerges with humble but determined vision on the other side. We give people the respect they deserve and together find our way to better solutions. Three ways of practicing respect—through listening, imagining and promoting rights—can help guide us toward the slow kingdom coming.

Listening Is Key to the Golden Rule

Recently a friend, Janet, told me how listening taught her more about the Golden Rule of respect. She's a grandmother whose hug envelops those she greets. Not long into a new year, I asked how her Christmas was. She said it was her best ever. She'd baked more than a few cookies, using eighty-five pounds worth of flour. She had baked late into weeknights and all weekend for two weeks. She gave the cookies to friends and then, not surprisingly, still had extras. She laughed at herself then told me more.

"I don't know how to put this," she said. "I'm there at church on Christmas Eve and the words are beautiful, the songs are beautiful, the story is beautiful. But I know them all. I don't know how to say this without it sounding wrong. It's like I need . . . I need a new story."

I understood her to mean that she wanted the story of God's being born into our world to be true not only in the sense of two thousand years ago, but here and now. She needed the story to come closer, the kingdom to come closer, so she could be part of it.

Her overzealous baking and undernourished spirit led to an epiphany. She went home after the unsatisfying baby Jesus celebration and rallied her family to put together boxes of the extra cookies. They spent the rest of that Christmas Eve, late into the night, driving around our town to six homeless camps that grow when people come south for the winter. (We live in Florida.)

By giving out cookies, she wanted to recapture some of the pure joy that her own grandma's cookies had given her as a child at Christmas. What a beautiful experience, I said, that she wanted something deeper and then found it by giving. Then I asked how people in the camps had received her gifts.

"Oh, some people welcomed us with a lot of thanks," she said, and then laughed. "Others told us what we could do with our cookies, and it wasn't something good!"

Then she told me about one particular encounter that night. She and her family parked beside a wooded area where they knew of a camp. But it was dark and the trees were thick. Then they saw a flicker. Like a match.

"But I didn't want to scare the person. And we'd just come from church. So," she said laughing, "I started moving into the woods toward the light saying, 'Be not afraid! Be not afraid!'"

An angel in pursuit.

The light she'd seen was a flashlight. The man holding it didn't turn off the light and disappear. Apparently he wasn't afraid.

"I told him I'd brought cookies. Then I asked his name, and he told me it was David. Like the star over the city of David. Can you believe it?"

"Would people be interested in cookies?" she asked David. "We could give them to you. Or people could come to our truck. Or we could take them to folks."

Honè.

"Are you part of a church?" David asked.

Feeling the dissatisfaction of the service she'd attended earlier that night and her need for the story to come to life outside the church building walls, she said, "No, I don't feel like I am right now."

"Yes, I think people would like it if you brought cookies to us out here," he said.

Respè.

"Can I bring my family with me?"

"Sure."

They followed David's flashlight (star) to a camp hidden deep in the woods. A fire burned in the center of camp, which hadn't been visible through the thick brush.

"Would you like a tour?" David asked.

He told her that about seventy people were living in the camp, but she only saw about forty. Apparently some had pulled back into the shadows, maybe feeling vulnerable as outsiders came. David told her that life just doesn't work for him out in the world. He was a Vietnam veteran and helps everybody follow camp rules, like if someone comes across food, it has to be brought back to camp and shared with everyone.

The evening, she said, then became a kind of twelve-step meeting around the fire, with everyone, including Janet's family, sharing and listening to each other's stories of addiction and loss. Then they prayed together, thanking God both for what they have and what they don't have.

Respect was given. A little trust was built through listening in a situation where there was legitimate reason for distrust on both sides (safety for Janet's family, a raid or betrayal of some kind for people in the camp).

Eventually, farewells were said. When it was done, nothing had changed. Not yet. It's still complex. The nostalgic joy of grandma's cookies wasn't simple to pass along. But it was a meaningful start.

I've been there. The heart is moved by compassion and gets a jolt of the adrenaline necessary to do something exciting and a little scary. Then comes the time to slow down enough to listen and give respect to one another, as was done here. The doors might start to open for more change, for lasting change, for a journey into deeper respect. But it takes time.

Right after college I had worked for a couple of years with refugees in Western Europe. Then, while studying in seminary, I'd spent a summer living with poor seminary students, eating the same boiled rice with watery tomato sauce twice a day, in the province of Karnataka in southern India. Then working in Albania, I had lived with a family in their simple home for four months. But I still longed for a deeper connection, for a deeper way to listen, as I started new work in Haiti.

When Shelly and I made that move thirteen years ago, within twenty-four hours we were in the countryside living with a Haitian family. The patriarch was essentially a subsistence farmer. For seven months we lived in a tiny room in their small tin-roof house with no running water and no electricity. I wrote about this experience in my first book, *Following Jesus Through the Eye of the Needle.* It was an attempt to be faithful to God and to my new neighbors where I was going to work.

Aren't there more sane ways to do it? This is a reasonable question for someone—for example, my father-in-law—to ask.

If one word could sum up why we chose this approach, it would be *respect.* We wanted to respect the people we were going to work with enough that we would go as learners. We wanted to focus on language and culture before wielding anything like power, because even with limited resources, those working in economically disadvantaged communities can have a lot of power in other people's lives. Our organization had a relationship with a small, Haitian-founded grassroots development organization in the nearby town. They had asked its members if they would be interested in receiving us (a way of saying *honè*). The Haitian organization thought it was a good idea that fit their cultural exchange goals with the community, so they found a highly regarded family in a nearby village who wanted to host us (a way of saying *respè*).

Shelly and I moved in and started a slow, sweaty, awkward, beautiful daily journey from sympathy to empathy, from charity to friendship. On this path of listening I've found two kinds of listening especially helpful for growing in the practice of respect.

First, listen incarnationally. It's important to *be with* and not go right into *doing for.* This was Shelly's and my experience with the family. This is among many things I've learned from my friend and colleague John Engle, who has lived in Haiti for most of the past twenty-three years. Listening incarnationally and attentively for many years, John can do effective education and community development and overcome challenges that would crash most projects.

A few years ago I got to spend time in the slums and red light districts of Bangkok with missionaries who have been called "new friars." They're good examples of a similar approach to listening incarnationally to people so they can work sensitively for justice. God came to us in the embodied Jesus, not via telegram or as a disembodied spirit. We shouldn't put ourselves in the God/Jesus role of trying to save other people. But in Jesus' incarnation, we find a theological compulsion for our love to be *with* instead of remaining *at a distance.*

We can learn a lot from a distance, but we also need to listen up-close. The way the new friars share life with people in difficult, marginalized communities is a radical example. The principle can also apply, for example, to how a suburban church needs to listen closely so they can be mentored by their partner ministry in the city. Does the church merely send money, just drop in to help or get more personally involved? How much time is spent in the city? And does the incarnation go both ways so that people from the city are coming to the suburb? We need to seek everyone's transformation together. Are questions being asked about what it means for a suburban church to truly be present in the city? Are difficult conversations held about race and money? Are some people moving from the suburbs to the city because they want to be part of God's kingdom coming in that place? And if you are part of this ministry, are you getting to know people in the city—so, yes, you're serving but also building relationships?

Second, listen to learn. North Americans often arrive in another country eager to solve problems. It is difficult for the pioneer spirit to be a patient learner, beginning with language, culture and history. This kind of listening was missing in the four young people who were working at the Cambodian orphanage (see the first chapter). But it's good to apprentice whenever we can. The organization Shelly and I went to Haiti with called our first seven months "An Apprenticeship in Shared Living." We want our personal doctors to have been residents first. We want our mechanics to be certified. In the work of justice we should be just as serious about listening to instruction. Wouldn't God's call on our lives include listening to wisdom already learned by the body of Christ? We should never force our solutions. If we enter carefully with the practices of attention, confession and respect, and if our help is welcomed (*honè–respè*), then we can listen together to discover how to partner for change. This work will then include listening to learn, step by step, along the way.[2]

The apostle Paul's conversion on the Damascus Road was instant, but it doesn't seem he was then instantly ready for the work of the gospel. In the three years before his recorded ministry started, Paul went to Arabia, perhaps for ministry but some scholars think this was for a time of preparatory listening to God.

N. T. Wright proposes that Paul may have been going through a recalibration:

> The God of Israel called me, like Elijah, to step back from this zeal and to listen to him afresh. When I listened, I heard a voice *telling me that the messianic victory over evil had already been won* . . . saved by grace and marked out by faith, apart from ethnic identity and works of Torah. I therefore had to renounce my former zeal, and announce the true Messiah to the world.[3]

If our zeal is to "go and help people," then, like Paul and like the grandmother giving out cookies, we may need to renounce our former zeal and have it transformed. This will largely happen through friendships and experiences with other people—through listening. Exchanging *honor* and *respect* at the threshold where we want to help gives us a chance to grow in the practice of respect.

IMAGINING TO AVOID CHEAP COMPASSION

In addition to listening, we need our imaginations to guide our practice of respect. In *The Cost of Discipleship*, German theologian Dietrich Bonhoeffer wrote about the dangers of cheap grace, which he defined as "the preaching of forgiveness without requiring repentance, baptism without church discipline, Communion without confession. . . . Cheap grace is grace without discipleship, grace without the cross, grace without Jesus Christ, living and incarnate."[4]

If we're unwilling to pay the cost of respect (through the practice explained in this chapter) in our work for the slow kingdom coming, we may find ourselves unwittingly engaged in cheap compassion, which, like cheap grace, isn't enough because we want to engage in real compassion, even if it costs more. But as we confess this vulnerability, we can find freedom to imagine ourselves in other people's shoes and thus deepen in our respect. As we read in the letter to Philippians, "in humility regard others as better than yourselves," which is a radical demand on our imaginations by the God who chose to be "found in human form" (Phil 2:3, 7).

Personal relationships are a primary way our imaginations are transformed so we can move from sympathy to empathy, from compassion to respect. This helps us to love our neighbors

> **Personal relationships are a primary way our imaginations are transformed so we can move from sympathy to empathy, from compassion to respect.**

as ourselves, which makes a rigorous demand on our imaginations. This doesn't mean that I should simply love you the way I imagine you'd want to be loved if our circumstances were reversed. Jesus is leading me to take love so seriously that I love you *as though you are you*, which is how I want to be loved *as me*. This means I need my imagination to be informed by you.

This has been part of the hope of short-term missions trips. Honor and respect can grow because we can then imagine what it is like to be in completely different circumstances when we cross racial, economic or national borders.

Short-term missions done well can transform our imaginations and change us for life, but when done poorly they are largely a failure of imagining: What's it like to be on the receiving end of these trips? They can then become cheap compassion and turn into poverty tourism, which exploits the very people we want to help. In the opening chapter, First Church wrestled with this when the main thing short-termers learned was "It just makes you so grateful for what you have" or "It puts life in perspective." If the primary takeaway of being with people who are suffering is that we feel better about our own lives, we are disrespecting them.

We can improve at practicing respect by imagining ourselves on the receiving end of these visits and asking ourselves a few significant questions.

How would I want to be visited? Respect is the guide. Our visiting must be characterized by dignity and humility, without patronizing. Visitors should come to learn, not to save. We should speak kindly of people and be gracious, engaged guests, and not see ourselves as tourists to be served. Because crossing cultures is complex, ideally these trips should be orchestrated by people who have long-term relationships with the community. Guests should remember that they are not visiting a movie set or an anthropology museum, which means we should ponder whether we should take photos of others. If so, we need to be sure we're getting permission, protecting minors, respecting dignity and thinking through the images we share. In the midst of travel we need to resist the temptation to release stress by dismissively saying how things could be done better with relative ease. Misunderstanding and discomfort is part of these trips, but imagining what it would be like on the receiving end can change the way we visit.

Would people do anything different after they saw my struggles and then returned home? Respect requires that we recognize our obligations (our due regard) to other people. This means our experiences must make a difference when we return home. We disrespect the people we visit if their suffering doesn't make any difference in choices we subsequently make with our lives. If our imaginations aren't awakened to the implications of justice, we might be more respectful by just staying home. At least the disrespect doesn't become personal. Respect means allowing the suffering of people I've met to shape how I give, what politics I engage in and how I spend money and order my ambitions.

Would people stay committed to helping my family and community? People are often gracious hosts and share the best parts of their lives with us when we visit. We thank them effusively for receiving us and say how meaningful it was. We think maybe in their beautiful smiles we see they've tapped into a secret happiness in the midst of punishing circumstances, which we wish we could find. But we shouldn't think that the stress of survival and watching their children suffer isn't as hard for them as it would be for us. We shouldn't take their generosity of spirit as an excuse to quarantine the unsettling parts of our experiences, the parts that demand more of us. If we slow down to reflect, we know that spending a week building a community center or holding babies in an orphanage or teaching English doesn't help systemic suffering. Imagine being on the other end of an intense week of fellowship in which people see your challenges, and then you never hear from them again. Whether we become long-term advocates for the people we visit determines whether we truly respect them or leave that respect behind as soon as we board the plane to home.

These three questions can awaken our imaginations and put a sort of *respect tax* on the people traveling from a position of privilege. They also reveal how practicing *confession* (in this case, privilege) can open our eyes to a more respectful approach. With slight variation, I think these three questions can also apply to visiting people who, for example, are different racially, economically or religiously. We should regularly cross all kinds of borders (God's kingdom does!) as we learn and seek justice, with an *honè–respè* approach.

The cultural gulf is wide between the white Christian Reformed Dutch members of Calvary Church in Michigan (see the chapter on attention) and the Haitians with African heritage and a deeply mystical culture. But the way Calvary has done short-term trips—starting with those first jubilee trips around the world—has awakened the congregation's imaginations to respond well to these three questions with respectful visits, long-term change in their own church and serious, ongoing commitment to the people they visit each year in Haiti.

My friend Jonathan Chan lives in Richmond, Virginia. His parents moved from China to the United States to attend university. A second-generation immigrant, he grew up between cultures and in a conservative church. In college he awoke to issues of reconciliation and justice through a campus ministry and a missions conference. Eventually that led him to choose to live, go to church and be part of a community working for reconciliation in his hometown, which has a four hundred-year history of racial, economic and political strife, including as the capital of the Confederacy in the Civil War. Slow kingdom coming indeed, but he wants to participate with respect in its coming.

Jonathan's church has its roots in a group of white and Asian American friends from a nearby university and a suburban church who wanted to get involved in an economically depressed part of their city. They connected with an African American leader who had lived in that community his whole life and had a vision for the area to be transformed. They listened so their imaginations could be shaped and then guide them with respect into this new neighborhood. The community leader became a kind of spiritual mentor for the folks who were moving in to get involved with issues like healthcare, after-school programs and affordable housing. A significant focus of these educators, doctors and business people was also to live in community with their new neighbors. John Perkins, a minister and civil rights leader, visited and said that for the community to really flourish they needed to become more deliberate about how they were involved with church in the neighborhood. So the African American elder, along with the group who moved to the neighborhood, started a church together. Faithful presence.

It's not all smooth, of course. A few years in several African American leaders of the church respectfully called the attention of one of the white ministers to how his leadership was making white culture dominant in worship and leadership. The pastor confessed his blind spots and began adjusting. Now he says that if people in the church are comfortable more than 75 percent of the time, then they're doing something wrong and letting one culture dominate more than it should. Challenges to reconciliation and justice remain, but the church and community keep informing each others' imaginations so they can keep pressing forward with respect.

Respect takes effort and discomfort. Respect is also the route to getting involved in each others' lives in ways that can be transformative.

In *Strive Toward Freedom,* Martin Luther King Jr. said in the wake of the Montgomery bus boycott, "Men often hate each other because they fear each other; they fear each other because they don't know each other; they don't know each other because they can not communicate; they can not communicate because they are separated."[5] We build bridges of respect by engaging with others deeply, with our lives and our imaginations.

PROMOTING RIGHTS TOWARD JUSTICE
We listen and use our imaginations to practice respect. The third essential ingredient to respect is promoting people's rights.

Economist William Easterly's book *The Tyranny of Experts: Economists, Dictators, and the Forgotten Rights of the Poor* points out that poor people's rights are abused not only by dictators but also by well-intentioned people seeking to help them.

The book makes the case that defending and promoting people's rights (that is, their freedom) is the most effective long-term way to achieve development. Confessing its discrimination, for example, against Native Americans, African Americans and women, we can still find *ideals* in the US Constitution to serve as a guide star: "We hold these truths to be self-evident, that all . . . are created equal, that they are endowed by their Creator with certain unalienable Rights."

When I talked with Easterly over tea, he told me his understanding has evolved.

> For me, this has been a long intellectual journey, from being one of the experts who was oblivious to the "rights of the poor" issue, to now criticizing those experts. In my development career, I worked closely at various times with autocratic governments. . . . I realized our attitude towards the poor is so often condescending and paternalistic. We think of them as helpless individuals. We don't respect their dignity as individuals.[6]

He continued, "The next step was not to just avoid paternalism or condescension but actually to go back to first principles and think about the rights of the poor and what role those rights play in development."

A strong, positive link between rights and development was also revealed in a fourteen-year study by sociologist Robert Woodberry published in *American Political Science Review.*[7] Woodberry looked at the link between missionaries and liberal democratization, and found that missionary activity (that wasn't financed by the colonizing state itself) often helped to advance widespread education and literacy, and helped protect native people from abuse by colonists.

Advancing people's rights in their societies is an essential part of respect and one of the clearest paths toward justice and development. We can think about the Bill of Rights and the right to freedoms like religion and expression. There is the democratic right to participate in shaping one's government. Property rights are important for healthy societies and economies.

The importance of rights applies to international development and the progress of nations. It also applies to our communities in tangible ways. In my church we were discussing the idea of respect as part of the work of justice, which led to considering the Black Lives Matter movement. In the midst of the many historical and social complexities, it seems one straightforward part of the movement is that the communities in Ferguson, Baltimore and across the country want to be treated like others, that the Golden Rule of respect would apply to black people in the same way it applies to white people. It's tragic and true that more than two hundred years after the constitution, there is still a need to fight for these kinds of rights to apply to *all*.

> The Golden Rule is simple, but it takes listening, imagining and promoting rights to live it well.

On a personal level, when we're working for justice we should be guided by people's rights. The Golden Rule is simple, but it takes listening, imagining and promoting rights to live it well.

• • •

The Hippocratic Oath, ethical guidelines for doctors to respect patients, was necessary because doctors have power over patients' lives. Likewise, working for the slow kingdom coming often includes a power differential between those serving and those being served. But whether we have more or less power, we're always invited to follow the Golden Rule. So a similar oath might help us along the way of respect:

A Golden Rule Oath for Respect

I will pay close attention to the implications of every word and act for justice, while acknowledging I can't know all the implications.

I will keep my eyes open to the damage I can do when I try to help others.

I will be an apprentice.

I will respect people in the way I visit, listen, begin partnerships, continue those relationships and share stories about my experiences with them.

I will do my best to understand other people's situations, while realizing I can never fully understand them or their circumstances.

I will stand up, to the extent it is wise and I am able, for the rights of those I seek to help and will challenge whoever or whatever encroaches on those rights.

I will apply Jesus' Golden Rule to all my work for the kingdom. First, with people being exploited. Then also with those who are making mistakes or are malicious. Always the goal is moving together toward God's kingdom through the ways of the kingdom.

I will submit my goals to the goals of people I'm trying to help. I will not play God in other people's lives but seek to humbly participate in God's story of bending the arc of history toward justice.

In Christ, we're invited into a lifelong practice of respect that, like the practice of confession, can keep healing us and opening our eyes to beautiful new kingdom possibilities.

The first year I was working in Haiti we were back in the United States on a staff retreat with Haitian and American colleagues. I led devotions one morning using *lectio divina* (divine reading). It's an approach to Scripture and prayer I'd learned in seminary that originated with monastic communities more than a thousand years ago. In one common version a short passage is read aloud several times. People are invited between readings to share what they hear God speaking to them and then to respond to God in prayer.

So I did this with about thirty colleagues. We translated into Creole along the way so everyone could participate. Afterward, a Haitian school principal told me we should try this in Haiti. So we did. Since then we've shared this with thousands of people, and I've come to realize the principal intuitively saw in *lectio divina* the three important elements of respect we've looked at in this chapter.

Listening. In a country where about half of people are illiterate, everyone would be able to listen. Listening should guide us in whatever ways we do justice.

Imagining. Everyone sits in a circle, and through the voices of Scripture, the Holy Spirit and each person in the circle all are invited to imagine more clearly the kingdom coming and how they can take part. Our imaginations can take us more deeply into respectful ways to love mercy.

Promoting rights. Whether someone in the group is an illiterate subsistence farmer or holds a theological degree, is a man or a woman, is in a cathedral or on rickety church benches over a dirt floor, the leader simply facilitates and each person is equally respected as someone sharing about their experience of God and life. We respect people's rights as part of walking humbly in the world with our neighbors and our God.

For eighteen years *lectio divina* has helped shape me and my understanding about the importance of respect in the work of justice. The people I'm with usually hear God much better than I do, and I'm grateful they let me sit in the circle with them. This relates to what Martin Luther King Jr. said in *Strive Toward Freedom* about the importance of people knowing each other. It also relates to the grandmother's experience after the cookies were eaten, when she and others sat around a fire at the homeless camp sharing honestly about life and growing in respect for each other. It relates to how we are guided by respect in the work of justice in our own community or when we travel abroad.

Now, I'm in Haiti about six times a year and I usually get to do *lectio divina* with people. Most visits I also stay for a night with the family my wife and I first lived with. Each time I travel down the dirt path to their *lakou* I pause to say *honè*, then wait to hear *respè*. The honor and respect keeps growing deeper. It's not perfect. I've had to learn a lot over the years. But it's a growing relationship of faithfulness to one another and to God.

We are encouraged in the practice of respect as we catch glimpses of Paul's beautiful advice to the community in Romans, "Love one another with mutual affection; outdo one another in showing honor."

PARTNERING

With Not *For*

*I always pray with joy because of your partnership
in the gospel from the first day until now.*

PHILIPPIANS 1:4-5 NIV

*True generosity lies in striving so that these hands—whether
of individuals or entire peoples—need be extended less and
less in supplication, so that more and more they become
human hands which work and, working, transform the world.*

PAULO FREIRE, *PEDAGOGY OF THE OPPRESSED*

I sat at a breakfast table in a nice Chicago suburb with a mom, dad and three kids. The dad takes the morning train to work at a downtown bank. Outside, the driveway leads to a small garage with a basketball hoop on it. Inside, we ate cereal, everyone a bit blurry-eyed.

Then Aimee, the mom, pulled a chart off the fridge and the kids prayed for the world with impressive depth and specificity. They had learned together about these situations and places. Chris and Aimee Fritz, who have been good friends of mine for more than twenty years, had both worked in ministries in Europe and locally. They care about the world. As a family they're figuring out how to care in the midst of busy lives and a consumer culture. Caffeine hadn't kicked in yet, but I got a jolt seeing them explore what it means to love the world faithfully as a family.

Their "family compassion focus," as they call it, started when their twins (a boy and a girl) were eight and their youngest daughter was three. The family had a bad Christmas experience: It should have been perfect, there were lots of toys, but the kids were dissatisfied and arguing soon after unwrapping the bounty. So the Fritzes vowed to change. They wanted to celebrate Jesus' birthday, not use Jesus' birthday to give themselves gifts.

After Christmas, they read Matthew 25 with their young kids to reorient themselves. That led to a baking adventure in the spring they called "Sprinkles of Hope." They sold sixteen hundred cupcakes to their neighbors, a baseball team and their school, which led to sending $2,600 to help a nonprofit in Uganda.

The following Christmas, before opening presents, they reviewed a binder that included everything they'd learned about orphans, Uganda and lessons about giving and helping well. Christmas day was joyful and meaningful because their year was oriented differently.

That night at Christmas dinner, their daughter Zoe asked, "So what's our compassion focus for next year?" Much like Pastor Wevers at Calvary Church, Chris and Aimee were thinking of this as a one-time reset. But the experience shifted their *attention* and moved them in a new direction.

They did family research for a week, and on New Year's Day they voted as a family to learn about and help with clean water. They read articles, learned about the issue and partnered with the charity Blood:Water. Through selling homemade crafts and lemonade outside Starbucks (with permission), they raised $20,000 to help others through this charity committed to providing access to water in Africa for long-term community development.

Their adventure has continued for four years. They have fun celebrating because anything Chris is involved with marries the silly with the serious. Aimee is a meticulous organizer. The kids research different helping opportunities that draw their attention. A boy's natural fascination with poop led to researching developing-world latrines. They're learning each country's history.

I've watched them continue to become better partners as they gain more experience and Zoe, Caleb and Greta keep growing in wonderful ways. Their experience leads us first to consider two regularly used approaches to *partnering* that have admirable aspects: (1) *rescue partnership*, trying to save other people, and (2) *fix-it partnership*, trying to fix other people's root problems. Sometimes we may find ourselves bouncing between them. I have. But ultimately both fall short as long-term models.

We'll then turn to how we can practice partnership in a way that most respects everyone involved: (3) *equal agency partnership*, supporting people's agency, that is, their ability to solve their own problems and create their own opportunities.

Finally, we'll look at how to best understand partnering in this slow kingdom coming: (4) *partnering together with God*, finding our true agency by participating together in the love and work of the trinitarian God.

•••

Rescue Partnership

Over the years, a few times after I confessed my compassion fatigue to people, I've been told a story that has also come to feel fatigued to me. It goes like this:

A man walking down the beach found many, many starfish on the sand. As he kept walking, he came up to another man, who was picking up the starfish and throwing them back in the water.

"What are you doing?"

"Throwing the starfish back in the sea. They'll dry out otherwise."

"But can't you see there are thousands and thousands of them? You'll never throw them all back in. You can't possibly save them all."

"No," said the man as threw another starfish back into the water, "but I just saved that one."

Experiencing versions of this story has kept me going at times, when I'm at a loss about the efficacy of our work for justice, when I'm overwhelmed by the big picture. I see change in one person's life, or I see one small way I can tangibly help. I give a family $100 and know it will help their kids eat this month. Such acts of rescue can be like getting hooked up to a respirator when a lack of hope makes the air too thin to breathe. I'm sure you've done these kinds of rescues too. Sending a check or giving online after a disaster. Giving money to someone homeless.

> The starfish story makes the act of helping someone seem easy and instant.

A "starfish rescue" partnership is fulfilling because it engages our best selves and answers the call of our faith. The problem with the starfish story, if it becomes the guiding metaphor for how we help people, is that it makes the act of helping someone seem easy and instant—but it's removed from any sense of context. There aren't many real-life cases where we can rescue someone in a miraculously simple way that will change everything for all time, like throwing a starfish back into the sea.

Child sponsorship is marketed as a starfish story. The sponsor is invited to rescue a child by posting a photo of the child on her refrigerator and having her credit card charged thirty dollars a month. (I've done this.) The sponsored child's family and community are often secondary or invisible. There is not much context given for the child's sacrificing parents, the sociological dynamic or the historical factors that made this child vulnerable. Sponsorship is a very effective fundraising approach among North American Christians because we want a clear, direct way to help. Of course, this is a good impulse of compassion. And there are times when it's necessary. After an earthquake or a tsunami, rescuing is in order. When a woman finally makes the courageous move to flee a situation of domestic abuse, at the beginning a starfish approach is crucial. But for the long-term it's also not enough.

In the starfish story I realized I subconsciously picture the hero as a blue-eyed, barefoot Jesus, with a well-trimmed beard and flowing robe as he throws starfish back into the sea. This can still inspire compassion, but as a guiding approach it puts us in danger of paternalism and codependency. It reinforces an unhealthy model in which we're more like parents than sisters and brothers. At first we think, *Wow, look at how we're helping them!* Years later we may think, *Wait, I thought I was throwing them back in the sea, but I keep giving and things aren't getting much better. I'd feel guilty not continuing to give— yet so many starfish are still on shore, including the one I already threw back in.*

FIX-IT PARTNERSHIP

This leads to our next approach. As we practice partnering, eventually the starfish approach starts to feel inadequate. Let's look at another story I've heard a number of times before.

Suppose you're having a picnic with friends on the bank of a wide river. You're at a bend with some rapids. Suddenly you see someone flailing in the water as he is pulled along in the river's flow, crying out, "Help! Help!"

You and your friends run over. One friend jumps in as another scrambles to find a branch to hold out for the person to grasp. You're finally able to pull the person to safety.

Moments later as you sit on the river's edge, everyone breathing heavily, you hear more cries of "Help!" You see another desperate person being swept down the river. Then another. You and your friends scramble to rescue each of them. You're helping some, but others are drowning. It's more than you can handle. And people just keep getting swept down the river.

Even though you're overwhelmed by those urgently in need, at some point you need to send someone *up river* to find out why people are coming down the river in the first place. Someone needs to try to fix the source problem.

In other words, at some point it's not enough to walk the beach and rescue an occasional starfish by throwing it back into the ocean. We have to ask why so many starfish are dying on the beach. Can marine biologists determine whether it was caused by a change in water temperature or a pollutant? When so many starfish are dying, it's not enough to help one at a time; we need to search for a more comprehensive solution. How can we keep the starfish from washing back on the shore again?

The story about going up river corrects the starfish story by speaking to the complexity of helping and to the importance of looking at root causes. This is a step of maturity and shows growth in how we practice partnership. Though often more complex and time consuming, addressing root causes of injustice is worth it.

However, we won't stop here but will continue to a third approach of partnering, because these first two kinds of rescue have an *agency* problem.

In both cases the starfish and the drowning people (or implicitly the helpless people up river) are portrayed as passive recipients of our help. We want to move beyond this to a model that better respects people as cocreators of their own lives with God.

EQUAL AGENCY PARTNERSHIP

My own understanding of equal partnership sharpened a few years ago when my Haitian colleague Enel Angervil and I were invited to present our work at a conference for hundreds of college students who wanted to start working for justice.[1] As we and another colleague, Jonathan Chan, ate together in a Japanese restaurant (one way Enel likes me to practice respect is by going to restaurants that serve rice), we thought about how we try to practice equal agency partnership.

While the first two approaches to partnership can be helpful, for long-term work we need to be guided by an approach that most deeply respects people's ability to find their own ways to flourish. Rescue or fix-it approaches are natural ways to start. (And I should say that the best disaster-response work I've seen actually applies the practices of this book as well.) But the following are ways we can continue to grow as partners who respect each other as equal agents partnering in the work of God's kingdom.

We listen humbly. We listen to understand and deepen in our respect of others. This is an ongoing aspect of partnering. A common vision of opportunities and obstacles, which is key for good partnering, emerges from this listening.

We're open eyed about the context. Since Enel and I work together in Haiti, it's important to reflect on how this partnership involves someone like me (with many built-in privileges) stepping into a context of hundreds of years of historical, emotional, psychological, economic and spiritual complexity and pain. In Haiti for example, five hundred years ago people of European descent (like me) started wiping out the indigenous population of Taíno; then four hundred years ago they started bringing slaves from Africa, who achieved independence 210 years ago. Since then the Haitians have faced two American occupations, the United States' backing a brutal dictator, and on and on. This is the context of our partnership that we need to be aware of and take into account.[2] If I don't learn and respect this, Enel could justifiably resent my presence in his country. And it would show I'm not serious about helping if I'm not willing to take context seriously and confess the dynamic it creates. I love that Chris and Aimee and their kids take months to read about and discover how their passion fits in with the needs of the people they would like to partner with. They learn history and research organizations before they start on their compassion focus projects.

We count the partnering cost. Enel chose the Scripture verse Luke 14:28—the same passage I had also seen him pick for a few other groups—to share with these young people at the conference. This is not the usual rousing call to justice or tear-inducing invitation to compassion: "Which of you, intending to build a tower, does not first sit down and estimate the cost, to see whether he has enough to complete it?"

Why this verse? Yes, we need to step out in faith to partner. But it's interesting that the theme at a conference like this typically invites people to take the risk of faith to try something radical—but the verse Enel (on the "receiving" side of partnerships) wanted to share is about the importance of counting the cost and being willing to follow through.

I've seen many people come and go in Haiti and other places. One American woman who Enel and I knew comes to mind. She came with initial support from her church and made many promises to help Haitians and to supporters back home. In about a year it all collapsed;

> **In living out our faith, it's important to be partners who listen and do what we say.**

her promises were broken. Her partnering was based on good intentions and naive hope, not on practicing confession and counting the cost. Despite the best of intentions, she wasn't treating people as equals, with the clear communication and commitment that follows through. There's a Creole proverb that says, "God does without speaking; people speak without doing." In living out our faith, it's important to be partners who listen and do what we say.

We prepare for angels and demons. Spiritually, we also should prepare for the fact that angels and demons will be part of our partnerships. In *The Contemplative Pastor*, Eugene Peterson says, "The happy result of a theological understanding of people as sinners is that the pastor is saved from the continual surprise that they are in fact sinners."[3] The same is true for partnerships: expect everyone involved to be a sinner, including yourself. When we keep this in mind, we can better prepare the way for all to do their best. We need to find ways for everyone involved to be transparent and accountable, especially around issues of money, sex and power. In formal partnerships this involves working for clear expectations and thinking through how partnerships can end well. A wise, diverse board of directors can help an organization with this. In a broader sense this book is about practices that prepare us to engage in a life of justice with an honest approach toward our angels and demons, our saintly and sinning selves. This is why confession is important to partnering.

We prepare the way for each other. Instead of "What would Jesus do?" a better guide for loving our neighbors might be John the Baptist's question, "How do we prepare the way for someone else's agency?" John was humbly committed to preparing the way for someone else to thrive, not to being the hero of the story. Enel, Jonathan and I try to find ways to help each other thrive, as we seek ways to help those we work with to thrive.

A first reading of Matthew 25 can jump-start us toward a starfish approach, but in fact it tells us we are to help prepare the way for Christ's presence by preparing the way of justice for others. Good work for justice involves helping others to become greater while we become less (see Jn 3:30). We serve as faithful partners preparing the way for other people's flourishing.

Marketing child sponsorships invites us to *rescue* a child in Bangladesh or Burundi, and a rescue-minded approach can get in the way of our maturing as partners. But the actual work on the ground is largely about *preparing the way* for that child through education or holistic community development. Partnerships like this encourage the child's agency, which ultimately improves his or her own community. In other words, the actual work, like I've seen groups doing in Haiti and other places, often takes a more mature, rigorous and helpful approach to partnership than the fundraising message.

Another example that comes to mind is International Justice Mission, which many of us learned about through their stories about dramatically rescuing those who were being trafficked in other countries for sexual slavery.[4] But that wasn't enough. Though their vision was holistic from the beginning, it deepened through their experience. They grew in how they operated and communicated about taking a comprehensive approach to transforming public justice systems. They started by giving starfish their lives back, one by one, and pulling people out of the (horrific) river of trafficking. Then they went up river to help. That has led them to a profound understanding of violence and how to be *equal partners* with others, empowering them to change their own countries so fewer people are exploited and more people flourish. When I was in Cambodia, for example, I learned how effectively IJM has partnered to prepare the way for Cambodians to reduce the commercial sexual exploitation of children.

We take the long view. If we're preparing the way for others, we can't force things. In our partnership, which stretches back over a decade, Enel has repeatedly said to me, "Okay, Kent. That might be a good idea. That might be a good person to work with. But let's wait. Let's watch. Let it develop, build trust and understanding. See how he does with a small responsibility first." And he's usually right. He still has to tell me sometimes, but less often now. You can have more patience if you're committed to persevere for the long haul. And with the right preparation it's possible to partner with short-term involvement that invests in a long-term, thoughtful strategy.

We build trust. Years after it happened Enel told me that when I first showed him our program budget, he didn't believe it was the real budget. He suspected it was a modified version. Only after four years of friendship and budgeting together, watching our program and the expenses, did Enel trust that he was dealing with our true budget. Transparency and honesty with each other create a cycle of trust, which leads to deeper partnerships and a sense of mutual

> **You can have more patience if you're committed to persevere for the long haul.**

responsibility. I find these two questions helpful to ask regularly: Where is a vulnerability that could lead to breaking trust? Where is an opportunity to build trust?

We spread credit around. When we honor each other's equal agency, it keeps a check on our ego; and if we're suffering from a lack of confidence, it reminds us that we are contributing. This leads to an experience of partnering that I found instructive both in the good it accomplished and in how tiny my role was.

Erwin is twenty-three. She lives in a patriarchal world, making her way in a seminary as a scholarship student in one of our programs. When I first met her, she was painfully shy. She could barely talk with me. A couple of years later, she confidently told me about a recent experience she had.

Erwin was leading a church Bible study on one of the taboos in Haitian culture and church, *restavek* children. (A *restavek* is a child or young person in Haiti who is living away from his or her family in domestic servitude, and is often exploited and abused.) An older woman started to cry and eventually told the group that her grown daughter had a *restavek* in her home who she didn't treat well at all. With Erwin helping her to reflect, the woman decided to convince her daughter to send the *restavek* back to her actual family, and not only that, but then to pay for that child to go to school while living with her own family.

I teared up as Erwin told me the story. It's amazing that a child who was in exploited bondage is now free. Hearts were transformed. So how did this door open? Everyone was partnering with equal regard for each other's agency.

Enel wrote the Bible study book that Erwin was using that day. Someone generously gave money so the books could be printed and Erwin could receive a scholarship. Erwin did the hard work of growing, learning and leading in faith. Our staff used their skills to develop the program. A Haitian printer printed the books at a discounted rate because he believes in faith working for justice. A cohort of Erwin's colleagues encouraged her to take the risk of leading this Bible study. The older woman was open to the Spirit, who convicted her. The young woman, the former *restavek*, has a much better life now, knowing some of the dignity and childhood that God has for her. And who knows how this young woman, who has since told us she is in school and much happier after escaping abuse, will prepare the way for others in the future?

This is a partnership story in which many people prepared the way for each other's gifts, and ultimately one young woman found freedom. Erwin and dozens of her colleagues keep working on this issue. Among colleagues who made change happen, my role was small. And they prepared the way for me to participate by teaching me the language, culture and much more.

Months after Enel and I presented these thoughts about *equal agency partnership* to college students, I recounted this story to an acquaintance in Florida. She seemed interested but isn't involved with any international justice work. When I finished, she paused so long that I thought she was working on a courteous way to avoid saying I'd just wasted ten minutes of her time. But then she said she was thinking about a difficult relationship with a family member who struggles with many serious issues in her life. She paused for a long time before saying these ideas on partnership had given her a vision for a new way forward in her relationship that had felt like it was at a dead end.

In Knoxville, Tennessee, I see my friend Daniel Watson practicing partnership in a similar way. (Daniel did the crazy mud race with me [see the first chapter], but don't hold that against him.) His attention to justice was shaped by growing up in a single-mother home with two siblings. Their lives were often a struggle. Ten years ago he and his wife founded a ministry to help single moms transition into better lives through their program and housing facilities. As I walked through their new facility with Daniel, it was profoundly encouraging to see in action what they call their five-way partnership between the benefiting families, mentors, staff, community partners and God. They see equal, respectful partnerships as key for the overall restoration and thriving of a family.

We have many partnerships in our lives. As we are faithful and just in them, we can help the kingdom to slowly come on earth as in heaven. We should see the practice of partnering as actually participating together in God's work.

PARTNERING TOGETHER WITH GOD

A few years ago I spent a couple of hours with fifteen Americans who were visiting Haiti. The group was four days into their trip and they had little experience in the country, which is among the more overtly Christian nations in the world. Conversations among strangers about Jesus happen regularly on public transportation.

I was sitting outside with this church group of Americans, two hundred feet from one church and a short walk from at least five churches along the village's main dirt road. I asked people to share their experiences so far. At least five people in the group said earnestly, "We just want to bring God and the good news of Jesus to the people of Haiti."

Here's the thing: God is already in Haiti. Has been for a long time.

If you think you're bringing God anywhere, you're on the wrong (starfish) trajectory of *for* instead of *with*. Whether we're in a Christian place like Haiti, a formerly oppressive anti-religious place like Albania, an isolated jungle village or an American suburb, we can't go where God is not already present.

So our deepest invitation to partnering is as equal partners who are together partnering with God. True partnership (cooperating) takes confession, attention, respect and sharing our power. Where there is a mutual desire to partner, we can practice *partnering together with God.*

When I was working with the refugee ministry in Europe, at one point I had to drive with a friend from Vienna to Timişoara, Romania, for a couple of days. We drove past apartment blocks that were still a communist shade of gray. I think it was 1994. We went to a department store where most shelves were bare. Out of curiosity I looked in a jewelry display case. There was a watch with an image on it that caught my eye.

I needed it, and I wasn't sure why.

I asked to hold it.

It strangely felt welcoming during a time when I was awkwardly trying to figure out where I was welcome.

I wanted to sit at the table situated in the image and listen and talk.

I wanted the poor kids who my friend Keren cared for in Timişoara, kids who slept outside and sniffed glue and had run away from the horrific state-imposed orphanages, to be welcomed at the table (on the watch) to eat from the simple bowl in the middle. They deserved to be there. The three people sitting there in the image, with their heads tilted slightly to the side, would welcome them.

The face of the watch, I found out later, was a famous icon of the Trinity created by the Russian painter Andrei Rublev. I think it was the first time I'd seen it. The effect on me was like the image's impact on millions since the fifteenth century. I bought it for a few dollars and put it on my wrist.

In the icon three people sit at three sides of a table. We see the icon from the fourth side—and we are welcomed into the empty spot. Or we can stay back a little and still feel welcomed. It's the scene from Genesis 18 where three angels visit Abraham outside his tent, and then a mysterious visit by the Lord occurs, which has been interpreted by Christians as a visit by the Trinity. It's also a portrait of the ultimate partnership we're welcomed into—into participation with God, and into participation with each other through God.

God is already here and there in Timişoara, Albania, Haiti, Bangkok, a Chicago suburb, wherever you are.

We're invited to cocreate (that is, to partner) with God and with each other in bringing God's kingdom on earth as in heaven. What does this scene with the three angel visitors tell us about partnering?

We're welcomed together. In Rublev's icon all three visitors are dressed in flowing robes, with halos around their heads and serene expressions on their faces. All their heads lean to the side. The mountain and tree behind them bend. This creates a peaceful yet dynamic circle effect of relationship. Stepping into partnership is to become part of something alive and in motion. And in the story of this icon, the trinitarian God, in whose image we are created, is shown to be a dynamic partnership. Partnership is at the essence of who we are as people and how we are to act in the world.

Early in our marriage I remember Shelly occasionally calling me "brother" when she was teasing me or trying to get me to do something when I was dragging my feet. Hearing that felt a little strange to me the first few times, probably because I was thinking so much about sex.

> **Partnership is at the essence of who we are as people and how we are to act in the world.**

But then I thought it was great because it was true—yes, our marriage is fundamentally a partnership together as a sister and brother in God. And with my weakness and failings, as I prepare the way for my son and daughter, it's powerful to think of my relationship with them as my brother and sister in Christ. With my wife, with my daughter and son, with Enel, in all my partnerships, we step up to that icon together—we move from other approaches of partnering to participating together in God's love—to hear what we're invited to next together.

Looking into this icon, we're invited into this circle with the triune God as we work together for justice. Our partnership isn't just between you and me, but between you, me and God, which changes how we think about treating each other, making goals, being mutually accountable and collaborating. Doing *lectio divina* Bible study together, which I mentioned in the previous chapter, is a way to be reminded of and instructed in respect and this kind of partnership. The group of Americans visiting Haiti wasn't bringing God. They were being welcomed to participate together in God's work with their Haitian sisters and brothers, to whom they owed honor and respect.

We're inspired but incredulous, believing and doubting. In the Genesis story Abraham goes into a holy hospitality panic, trying to get freshly baked bread for the visitors. As we practice *attention*, part of what we're doing is watching for when God walks through the room or stops by for dinner. Abraham honors God's presence. Serious, holy business is at hand.

But I love that in the back left corner of the icon is Abraham and Sarah's home. We can't see her (I've looked closely), but just inside the door is Sarah. When the visitors announce that she and her husband, at their shriveled old age, would have a baby, she laughs. That laugh merits sainthood. The Trinity shows up on the doorstep and Sarah's doubt makes her laugh out loud. We have room to doubt big and hope big for the amazing to happen in our partnerships with God and each other. Honesty about all of this helps. "If I have found favor with you . . ." (verse 3), Abraham says to the visitors. That is an important *if* of humility and doubt and faith.

We're to be wise. Sarah's skepticism also alerts us to the need for wise welcoming. God's loving capacity to welcome everyone at that table is infinite. We mortals have to be open to new possibilities and guided by grace, but also aware that our capacity isn't infinite. As Proverbs 29:24 says with a punch: "To be a partner of a thief is to hate one's own life." Partnering takes giving of ourselves but avoids self-destruction.

We're to create. Why did God show up? To deliver news that Abraham and Sarah are going to create something beautiful together. Partnership is the opportunity to create, in the broadest sense of the word, something you couldn't create on your own.

It won't be easy, but it can be good. God visited to prepare the way for them: "Believe it or not, here's what is coming next." In the partnership God would make it possible, but they would be responsible. This can be creating a child or a nation. It can be creating the possibility to elect a more justice-minded politician. It can be doing a new church project with the local homeless family center. It can be creating through art or tutoring or a thousand things.

When we practice partnership this way, we can move from doing things *for* other people to doing them *with* each other. We shift from thinking we're taking God somewhere to instead participating where God is already creating and sustaining, even if there are few signs.

There are many kinds of partnership in our lives. Some partnerships are briefly shared with provisional commitments and others we commit to for life with vows before God. In all of them, we should stay grounded in how God interacts with us. God created and sustains us—but we're not living in a Four Seasons Hotel with God delivering room service specified to our desires. There's a sense in which we are, with God, cocreators of our reality in a divine-human partnership. God created the animals; Adam named them. And then Jesus, God with us, came to show love and invite us to participate in salvation now and forever. God is, we believe, a mysterious partnership of Father, Son and Holy Spirit (Creator, Redeemer and Sustainer). To practice partnership, in the words of the classic book by seventeenth-century monk Brother Lawrence, is to practice the presence of God.

A popular quote in grassroots justice circles, attributed to the aboriginal Australian leader Lilla Watson, says, "If you have come here to help me, you are wasting your time. But if you have come because your liberation is bound up with mine, then let us work together." Yes, instead of partnering *for* we do better to partner *with*. In different circumstances this will look differently, and there can be starfish and up-river moments, but we should always be oriented toward partnerships that are *with*.

When Chris came from Chicago to Haiti with me seven years ago, Aimee was pregnant with Greta. The connection wasn't great, but we could make quick cell phone calls from where we were staying in the village with the family Shelly and I first lived with. Chris talked with Aimee on the phone for five minutes. Then he walked over and didn't look good. He said there were serious pregnancy complications. Now he's so far away. I explained to the grandfather in Creole. The grandfather, Pere, said we needed to pray.

The whole family gathered on the porch of this small tin-roofed home. And they prayed. Especially Pere. He prayed and prayed in Creole. Chris couldn't understand anything, but of course he also understood everything.

Aimee's health improved. Greta was born and is vivacious and helps lead the "family compassion focus" charge. And of the dozens of visitors I've introduced Pere and the family to over the years, Pere asks about Chris more than anyone. And Aimee and Chris feel like Greta's life was mysteriously, tangibly blessed because of Pere's prayer. Chris wasn't merely there to help the family to have better lives, and Pere wasn't merely trying to help Chris understand Haiti better. On the porch we came into that circle, like in Rublev's icon, and partnered with God together to seek the kingdom coming on earth as in heaven.

TRUTHING
Hard Thinking and Feet on the Ground

You will know the truth,
and the truth will set you free.

JOHN 8:32 NIV

The truth will set you free.
But not until it is finished with you.

DAVID FOSTER WALLACE, *INFINITE JEST*

L ove without truth is a boat without a rudder. Our hearts can be big and compassionate but won't be steered to help like we should. On the other hand, truth without love to act on it floats inert, as a kind of shiny trophy indifferent to the needs of the world.

When love and truth work together, however, that's when we're moving in the right direction toward God's kingdom with a formula that looks like this:

Truth multiplied by love equals a more just world.

This *formula of flourishing*—by which we see people and creation flourish as God wants—leads toward justice. But it is a challenge to connect love and truth. "To see what is in front of one's nose needs a constant struggle," said George Orwell.[1] It's a worthy struggle because the hope and the stakes are so high in this slow kingdom coming. We're vulnerable to complacency or hurting people or at least not helping them in the most effective ways when they need our best effort. How do we ensure truth is the rudder that steers our love? The practice of *truthing* gives us the opportunity to love our neighbors with our very best stewardship.

To learn more about this practice, I stepped off a dock in a swamplike area into what looked like a time machine. A tangle of tubes and wires and a huge fan seemed put together by a mad scientist in his garage. It was actually an airboat owned by the South Florida Water Management District. I was going to spend the day with a scientist, Lawrence Spencer, on the Kissimmee River in an area sometimes called the Northern Everglades.

> The practice of *truthing* gives us the opportunity to love our neighbors with our very best stewardship.

I wanted to learn about this scientific process called *truthing* or *ground truthing*, which involves checking big-picture assessment (in this case, aerial images) against the reality on the ground. For example, researchers take satellite images of a geological formation and then go to see how accurately it describes the makeup of the rocks under their feet. Though it generally refers to a geological or an agricultural research process, truthing is also a crucial practice for the work of the slow kingdom coming.

On this day Lawrence was studying vegetation growth in the flood-plain wetlands of the Kissimmee River. In the 1950s the Army Corps of Engineers turned this winding river, with a flood plain three miles wide, into one deep, straight canal running down the center of the state. Soon after the canal was built, people realized it was an ecological disaster. The decades-long process is now underway to restore the river to its previous state, which is better for the environment, for wildlife and for the drinking water of millions of people in Florida.

As we sped on the airboat/time machine through the canals toward the flood plain, alligators slipped into the water. Big ones. I've seen a few movies with airboats that go back into narrow swamplike canals. They always include close-ups of alligators slipping underwater; the next ten minutes of the movie don't go well. But our task seemed pretty safe as Lawrence focused on three kinds of grass—maidencane, para and West Indian marsh grass. Maidencane is thought to be best for the local ecology, and the other two may be damaging. Truthing is vital because they can see where grass is growing in the aerial views, but they can't tell which of the three species it is until they examine it up close.

A similar process is important in the slow kingdom coming— an ongoing back and forth between the big picture and feet on the ground.

For example, if the prosperity gospel sneaks through our theological gates, then we should practice truthing to reveal its false promises, which exploit people. The slow kingdom coming can't flourish by planting a $300 seed offering, as nice and easy as that might sound. That is the temptation of a false shortcut toward a more just world. Truthing should lead to protecting people from the kinds of temptations that are especially used on those who are vulnerable, because they need more flourishing in their own lives. It's vital to have our feet on the ground.

As another example, a friend who works at a charitable foundation told me about a grant given to help a ministry build a community center in Bolivia. The building project was a good strategic idea. A report came with a nice photo of the completed building that was now going to help many people. One of the foundation's staff looked at the photo and thought something looked slightly off. They investigated. Eventually they figured out the community center had been photo-shopped in. It was never built. In the most basic sense of stewardship, we should practice truthing to confirm that money given to help our neighbors does what it's said to.

When I was in Cambodia earlier this year, an expat told me about a Cambodian pastor he knows who had two church signs. When one group of American visitors came, the sign out front said Christian Missionary Alliance. When a group from the other denomination visited, the pastor would switch to the sign that said Church of God. From a distance it's hard to know the truth on the ground. (It's sometimes hard up close too.)

And that's relatively harmless compared to a much worse failure of truthing in Cambodia. Earlier I mentioned the story of Westerners who had opened orphanages with good intentions in a place where children had much need. I was also told surveys eventually found that about 80 percent of children in Cambodian orphanages were not actually orphans. Parents, struggling with poverty, thought that in order to get better care and better education their child would benefit by living in a foreign-funded orphanage.

Over time studies in different countries have made it clearer that raising children in orphanages should be a last option, not a first. Simultaneously, the big picture revealed that the wave of orphanages actually created incentives to break up families who could have stayed together. As these things start to become clear, our love has to be guided by truth and move us to change. Fortunately, a number of groups (Cambodian and foreign) are shifting their focus. I talked with an American woman who has worked in Cambodia for twenty years and raised her children there. She started working in a missions orphanage but shifted in the past decade to facilitating a Cambodian system of foster and kinship care. I had the chance to visit a sixty-seven-year-old grandma who is raising some of her grandchildren through this kinship support. Circumstances are challenging, but they're making it as a family instead of being separated and the children being institutionalized. Seeing the resilience and love of the grandma, and the courage and faithfulness of this American woman who was guided by truth to change, is inspiring.

"Work out your own salvation with fear and trembling," says the apostle Paul (Phil 2:12). We should work out our compassion with fear and trembling too, because the stakes are so high for our neighbors as we live out the Golden Rule. When we practice truthing, we are humbled and kept in check. It keeps us learning and accountable to the people we serve and partner with. We're taken below the surface of things to deal with reality and to keep adapting to the best approaches.

And while fear reminds us of the stakes, the purpose of this practice is for truth to be guided by love. So then we actually leave fear behind because "there is no fear in love, but perfect love casts out fear" (1 Jn 4:18). We are freed from the paralysis of fear into following truth. This is the practice of seeking to perfect our modest love, even though we never achieve it. When it's done along with the other practices, the promise of truthing is to be freed from complacency and from fear.

As churches, nonprofits, communities and individuals, we can avoid hurting a community we sincerely want to help. We can find that change isn't threatening but actually frees us to learn and move beyond incorrect assumptions and toward more effective stewardship. As we zoom in and out and adjust our approach along the way, we can embrace the fact we'll be changing, adapting and learning from our mistakes. We can continue to be set free from fear to improve at loving our neighbors.

PERSONAL TRUTHING

I only found a name for it recently, but the practice of *truthing* has shaped my life. I love ideas and theory, but go crazy if they don't become practical. But then I also get easily disheartened doing practical work without knowing whether it's making a big-picture difference.

I was fortunate to see examples of truthing early in my justice work from people like Scott McCracken. Right after college, when I was working for a refugee ministry in Europe, Scott was a colleague in Athens. He was about ten years older than I. He has a great sense of humor and an intense approach to life.

Scott lived in an apartment with his wife and three young kids. I stayed with them a couple of times. He had developed a vibrant center for refugees to access helpful services and find a supportive community.

Scott's work was informed by spending two weeks living on the streets with the refugees, one week during summer and the other in wintertime. Scott slept each night in a public park with about two hundred refugees, mostly from Afghanistan and Iran. Similar to the refugees, who walked everywhere, he didn't wear great shoes and got blisters. During the winter week he purposely didn't take a heavy jacket and was cold most of the time, like many of them. He took eight dollars with him, enough to pay for the bus ride home. He visited the soup kitchens the refugees visited.

Scott did this so he could gain new insight into what was and wasn't helpful to people he was serving. It was done within a long-term commitment, not as poverty tourism. Scott already knew the big picture, but this practice of truthing made him better at responding to practical needs. He had taken the practices of *respect* and *listening* and embodied them with a specific purpose. He knew about the lack of warm jackets but hadn't understood how hard it was to bathe. After the experience he found a way to provide showers, for which the refugees were grateful. The truthing experience also kept transforming him as someone who, even deeper in his bones, was committed to find the best ways to help.

There is a tradition of this in journalism and literature. A classic example is Upton Sinclair's *The Jungle*, which exposed conditions of the meatpacking industry in Chicago in the early twentieth century and led to changes in federal legislation. Another example of personal truthing is in the book *Nickel and Dimed*, in which the author Barbara Ehrenreich chronicled her experience trying to survive at jobs like waiting tables and working at Walmart. This approach can turn an aerial view (living on minimum wage is surely hard) into a ground-level view (there's almost no way someone can escape poverty in that situation). My first book can be read partly as an experience in truthing, when my wife and I lived with a family in Haiti. That experience has led to lifelong friendships and has informed and improved my work every day for the past thirteen years.

More recently I've seen the group Sanctuary do this in Toronto. Their ministry is rooted in twenty-five years of deep relationships in the downtown community, serving homeless and marginalized people in the area. They've filled in gaps by providing community and social services. They practice truthing by being friends, by being out in the street, like Scott did in Athens. In their small clinic they told me how they learned through friendships about the gaps in medical care that they could fill for the people they serve.

They also help quite wealthy suburban Toronto churches learn about ministry in urban Toronto. Sanctuary does a "street orientation" (a brief apprenticeship in truthing) so, for example, suburban teenagers can learn from people who live on the streets, spend time with people they're usually isolated from, break down stereotypes and better understand how wealth and poverty and privilege and pain function in their city.

Whether through reading or our own experiences, truthing should move us as individuals from abstract acknowledgement of injustice to wanting to make a change and then restlessly searching for the best ways to make that change happen.

DATA TRUTHING

Individual truthing is essential, but the practice shouldn't stop there. When we are able to check ideas with a large sample of what happens on the ground, we often learn a lot. In biblical language we practice truthing so we can better see what acts of love are actually bearing fruit.

When Lawrence would stop the airboat based on GPS coordinates, he would lean over the edge to closely observe the stem, blades and flowering seeds to see what kind of wetland grass we were looking at. Back at the office Lawrence would later compare this to mapping with

> **We practice truthing so we can better see what acts of love are actually bearing fruit.**

the aerial images. The work, he said, could get tedious. But it's essential to evaluate the outcomes of the Kissimmee River project for Floridians who are paying for this with their tax money.

My brother-in-law, Chris Blattman, does evaluation for justice-related work on a larger scale than individual truthing. He is an economist, political scientist and a professor at Columbia University. He is part of a new generation of social researchers evaluating interventions to help people. Sometimes these studies confirm what we've long believed. Other times they turn our expectations upside down, as when studies started to show microfinance loans are not necessarily a magical cure to lift people out of poverty, as was once suggested.

This research is often done through randomized controlled trials, similar to study trials of pharmaceutical drugs. For example, Chris worked with 999 poor young men in urban slums in Liberia, many of whom deal in petty crime and drugs. There are high-risk young men like these in cities around the world, and governments and communities are unsure how to help them, or at least keep them from harming others. Chris has been working with the government and the aid community to test different approaches.

His team offered half of the 999 young men participation in life-skills therapy to help them improve self-discipline and self-image. To participate in this program, the men drew lots. A couple of months later, when that therapy was over, the men drew lots for a no-strings-attached cash payment of $200 (so they're receiving free cash instead of a microfinance loan, which would have to be repaid). This means that a quarter got therapy, a quarter got cash, a quarter got both, and a quarter didn't get either. Why do this? Because it wasn't clear which interventions, if any, would work.

They followed the men for a year and studied the results, which revealed that these young men managed their money well, even if they didn't get the therapy. They also found that the men who received the therapy fought less and committed half as many crimes, with the more lasting impact for those who received both the training and cash. Cash alone had a good but temporary effect, helping the men eat and live a little better for a while, and do a little business.

In other places Chris's studies have found that simple cash handouts have lasting effects. In a study with extremely poor and war-affected women in northern Uganda, he and his colleagues found that $150 in cash plus five days of basic business training and supervision helped them double their income in eighteen months because they became small traders. Providing ongoing supervision helped a little, but not enough to justify the high cost when compared to just giving more poor women the money that the supervision would have cost.

Chris and his colleague Paul Niehaus wrote about these types of cash transfers in "Show Them the Money" in the journal *Foreign Affairs*: "These days, it's about providing evidence of change—especially change that justifies the price of bringing it about."[2] Microfinance loans or an extensive training program paired with giving away a cow may be too expensive to administer for results that don't necessarily justify the amount of help they ultimately give. Experiments like this with cash transfers are an example of truthing (seeing what difference this idea makes on the ground) to evaluate stewardship of our unfortunately limited resources for loving our neighbors.

Okay, I got a little technical here. Why should we care? The resources and expertise to do these kinds of studies are far beyond most of us. Still, they're an example of the kind of seeking that is critical. Why? God has given us the responsibility to be good stewards as we partner with our neighbors for change. We're limited in our understanding and always have room to improve. With respect for the people involved, we should seek ways, such as these interventions and evaluations, to learn how to get better at helping each other to flourish. We practice truthing.

We've been trying this on a smaller scale in Haiti. A colleague has been surveying how training can shift church attitudes and behavior around the issue of *restavek* children. We know the difference a young woman like Erwin can make in one *restavek*'s life, as we saw in the chapter on *partnering*. But we need to keep learning the most effective way to help more broadly. My colleague Jonathan taught Erwin and her colleagues how to use tablet computers to do surveys. We work with an American PhD in social science to analyze the data. We still have lots to learn, but this helps us keep improving.

In the Ugandan study, Chris overturned conventional wisdom—that it's a bad idea to just give poor people cash—by truthing that takes observation to the next level of obtaining on-the-ground, quantifiable data. If we see charity broadly through paternalistic eyes that aren't challenged in ways like this, we'll misinterpret what we see and discount people's desire and ingenuity to better their own lives. We'll miss out on possibilities of *equal agency partnering*. The cost and the opportunity lost are devastating for everyone involved. On the other hand, when we find new insights into how to improve at the work of justice, it can make a life-changing difference for millions of women and men, girls and boys.

To run an evaluation program like this requires a lot of expertise and money, but all of us should be cheering them on, and the organizations we support should be learning from them and from other evaluation methods. We don't need more data just for data's sake. We practice truthing for love's sake. How exciting that we can find ways to test how effectively our love for our neighbors makes a difference in their lives.

> **Truthing is always hungry to learn more in service of love.**

So, we seek to learn from each other what works well. We find freedom from the fear that we might be wrong and embrace the fact that we *are* likely wrong to some extent and want to improve. We learn the history of the places where we want to help and take in all the information we can. We collaborate with people who have different perspectives to help guide us toward the best ways forward—people who are doing hard thinking and people with feet on the ground. Truthing is always hungry to learn more in service of love.

INCREMENTAL TRUTHING

When everyone is citing data and there is a study for everything, this can produce anxiety or tempt us to ignore the importance of understanding the results of our efforts. Truthing offers a better way forward. Truthing is freeing because we understand it as an iterative process toward love and improving step by step. We don't have to be paralyzed because we don't need perfect knowledge. Instead, we keep learning and adapting as we zoom in and out along the way (and as we grow in the other four practices). We don't ignore truth, because we want the faithfulness of our work to be accompanied by fruitfulness. That is, we want to see that our love is making an ever-increasing difference in people's lives. And we don't have to (pretend to) have perfect knowledge, but can humbly confess that we're learners partnering with a commitment to improving together.

I want educators in my kids' school and in the state and federal governments to be truthing so theory and practical experiences are in conversation to keep the quality of their education improving. We don't want people stuck in unfruitful old methods. We don't want teachers who are uninformed of the best new theory. And we shouldn't want theorists who aren't learning from real-life testing in the classroom. For educators as for justice we want the best minds and the best practitioners, both the aerial and on-the-ground perspectives, working together to help us keep improving incrementally.

We're called to love mercy. We're also called to love God with all our minds. We confess that we don't know the whole truth, so we're humble. All this is part of the incredible invitation we each receive from God to participate in the coming of the kingdom as we love our neighbors.

Recently, I started working on a new project that has provoked me to think about truthing—why it's important, why it's complex, why it should keep us both humble and motivated, and why the process is incremental.[3] I learned about six building blocks of a thriving community: the True (human knowledge and learning), the Good (social mores and ethics), the Beautiful (creativity, aesthetics and design), the Prosperous (economic life), the Just and Well-Ordered (political and civic life), and the Sustainable (natural and physical health).

What a great list. I love how we can look at it and each find areas where we can make our own small contributions and improvements as we contribute, learn and improve. At the same time, seeing the big building-block picture like this also reminds us of the complexity. There is no one single study, no new data analysis, no one breakthrough that will lead everyone to the promised land. Clearly this truthing process of both an aerial view and on-the-ground experience is essential to grow these building blocks in ways that make more of a difference for people in a community.

For example, when the institute looked at Portland as part of their thriving cities study, they learned about an initiative to put in more bike paths in the city. At first glance this seems like an easy justice win. Who, other than oil and car companies, could be against bike paths, which will encourage exercise and are good for the environment? But when the project was underway, issues came up because of historical tension and political factors with the African American community. Oregon's racial history is sordid. I thought of it as a progressive, liberal utopia because of, well, the *Portlandia* TV series. I wasn't taught that Oregon was founded as a racist state that, on its entry into the Union, forbade black people from living, working or owning property there. Of course, significant progress has been made since (which would have been, in part, a truthing process of changing ideas and policies and also looking at the effects on people's lives). But apparently when these bike lanes were proposed, which would have cut through black neighborhoods, some people started calling them "white lanes" because of who they would primarily benefit.

Justice is not always simple. Clearly, thriving for *everyone* in a community requires respect and partnership, confession of the past and truthing that takes both a *sky downward* view (city planning toward ideals) and a *ground upward* view (listening to the neighborhoods that would be affected) and goes both wide and deep. The conversation extended wider. Partnerships were built. Respect took a step forward. Some bike lanes were built. Everything is connected. In this case, environment, health and racial justice needed to be considered. Not everything was solved, but from a distance it seems a step forward was taken.

The bike lanes illustrate that what each of us sees is limited. There is plenty of work still to be done after having a good idea of how to help. Multiple perspectives and friendships help us understand and contribute within the complexity where God has placed us. The Spirit can move through all these areas, as well as individual lives, in transforming ways that are hard to understand or quantify. In truthing, we can confess this mystery as we take responsibility for our part.

Each of us can be a small but essential part of truthing, just as we've seen with Lawrence Spencer (studying grass on the Kissimmee River), Chris Blattman (analyzing cash transfers), educators in my kids' classrooms, and you as you help a church program serve people a little better this week than it did last week.

Jonathan, who I mentioned earlier is involved in a church focused on reconciliation in Richmond, recently got married. His wife, Caitie, works for a national organization focused on housing and banking in poor communities. They build regional coalitions of groups across the United States, work closely with banks and have influence at the federal policy level. One issue they work on is housing for low-to-moderate income people. Gentrification can sweep through a community and make people's own neighborhood unaffordable to them. Parts of Jonathan and Caitie's own neighborhood is starting to experience this. So Caitie is able to connect people with experts on issues like protecting or creating affordable rental properties in their community. And what she learns in day-to-day life with neighbors helps her better understand coalition building. Her work and her neighborhood have become part of a dynamic practice of truthing.

What a beautiful practice this is: humbly seeking truth for the healing of our world, step by step, in order to become more like the kingdom. As we practice submitting to the truth, being taught the truth, being led by the truth and being shaped by the truth, we learn how to better love our neighbors.

• • •

Truthing is part of all the practices in this book: *attention* (desiring to know the truth), *confession* (opening ourselves to hard truths), *respect* (giving respect often leads to hearing more of the truth) and *partnering* (which then helps us to hear and act on those multiple perspectives on the truth).

On the Kissimmee River project, we pulled into another section of wetland grass. Lawrence leaned over the side to see what kind of grass it was. He recorded the data, which he would also use for next month's aerial photos. He's hoping to figure out how to identify the three different grass species from the new

aerial photos, which will help them track the health and development of this complex ecosystem. The process is ongoing, back
and forth between *sky downward* and *ground upward*.

When he was done, we put our earplugs back in and he fired
up the airboat. But we only moved forward a few feet. He tried
again. We were stuck. He got out. The grass was thick and the
water was shallow. He trampled it down. We tried again. I got
out and trampled with him. I didn't say what I was thinking: this
seemed too thick for an alligator and I was glad he had said
earlier that the pythons in the Everglades hadn't been seen this
far north yet.

Everything was quiet. After a few minutes the frogs restarted
their grunting and the birds came out from hiding and started
singing. We could then better see the complexity because we
were taking time on the ground, a reminder as we practice
truthing that our presence can effect what we see around us.

Finally, he cranked the fan all the way up while I stood on the
grass and pushed the side of the boat. It started moving. I pushed
along and sloshed through grass and water and then jumped in.
We were off again.

Truthing involves getting stuck. Coming to our wits' end.
Needing to help each other out. Truthing leads us to be per-
sistent but patient. It's a practice that asks us to push into complexity, seek clarity and yet accept ambiguity. We receive failure
as grace. We pray. We evaluate. We discover new ways to help
each other. We work by faith and by sight.

Jesus said, "The truth will set you free." David Foster Wallace
wrote in his novel *Infinite Jest*, "The truth will set you free. But
not until it is finished with you."[4]

Indeed, we don't want truth to be finished with us. We want
our lives to be shaped by truth, though the process is not always
gentle or pleasant. We practice truthing because it helps us to

be good stewards as we work for transformation of the world with our neighbors. We practice truthing because whatever we follow is what we're transformed by—and so we want to follow truth and follow the One who is truth, who is life.

Jesus is, in a way, where the *sky downward* and the *ground upward* meet. From the omnipresent, seemingly *airlike* state of God, Jesus was born into straw and muck and walked with dusty sandals on the ground. He pressed through a crowd with a woman whose bleeding wouldn't stop. He touched the dead eyes of a blind man. In the past we kind of had an aerial view of God—a satellite image that was good and loving, but also distant and intimidating. Then God came close. Thomas, who was truthing on behalf of all of us, wanted to put his hand in his side (Jn 20:27-28), an on-the-ground experience.

Truthing, as a practice, does not make truth an inanimate thing we can hold and control. Instead it's a word of active following after what Jesus said, "I am the way, and the truth, and the life" (Jn 14:6). We follow, seek from every angle, correct, contemplate and dig. Blaise Pascal wrote that one shouldn't wait to believe before going to church or participating in worship. Instead he advised participating in the life and practices of faith to see if they bore fruit, if they shaped one's passions and desires, which was part of seeing whether one would believe.[5] In other words, don't be content with taking a proverbial satellite photo and decide on that basis it doesn't make sense.

How can you do truthing without adding to your already full to-do list? As you're able, visit and get involved personally where you give. Find ways to ask those who benefit from the services and gifts how it's going, how things could be better. When you pay attention to and respect them, there's a better chance you'll get real answers. Be willing to accept facts, even if they're inconvenient. Be willing to accept that data and studies are provisional, and keep learning. As we practice truthing, we're served well by a mindset of improving, not of proving.

Find a wise way to visit that "bad part" of town and discover if it's really as bad as people say. Building relationships with those on public assistance will give us a better understanding of what life is like for people in that situation, which can inform the sky downward perspective of how to help. Getting to know

> Truthing can be an encouraging, enlightening part of your daily participation in the work of God's kingdom.

people who are homeless may shatter stereotypes, spark compassion and give insight on how better to help. All of this may include taking more time to walk around your community (car culture keeps us isolated from each other and from knowing the reality of even our own communities). Truthing can be an encouraging, enlightening part of your daily participation in the work of God's kingdom—it can be part of how love casts out our fear.

It's vital for us to enter into the truth of other people's lives. We'll see the world differently. One of the dangers of even relative wealth is being isolated from the experience of others and thus slightly numbed to the urgency for justice. As followers of Jesus we're compelled to be friends with people on the margins, which is part of our practice of truthing. That's ground upward. Then we pay attention to the best aerial thinking so we can practice good partnering for change.

Truthing leads us out to discover what's there. In humility we know we need a feedback loop of multiple perspectives. We seek to understand the world around us and within us. Remember: truth multiplied by love leads us toward God's justice.

PRACTICING FAITHFULLY EVEN WHEN WE'RE OVERWHELMED

Seek first the kingdom of God.

MATTHEW 6:33 (NKJV)

I believe that we learn by practice. Whether it means to learn to dance by practicing dancing, or to learn to live by practicing living, the principles are the same. . . . One becomes in some area an athlete of God. Practice means to perform over and over again, in the face of all obstacles, some act of vision, of faith, of desire.

MARTHA GRAHAM, *THIS I BELIEVE*

As a young man, the Greek writer Nikos Kazantzakis spent a summer touring monasteries. In *Report to Greco* he recounts a conversation along the way with an elderly monk.

"Do you still wrestle with the devil, Father Makários?" he asked the monk.

"Not any longer, my child. I have grown old now, and he has grown old with me. He doesn't have the strength . . . I wrestle with God."

"With God!" Kazantzakis exclaimed in astonishment. "And you hope to win?"

"I hope to lose, my child," the old monk replied, "My bones remain with me still, and they continue to resist."[1]

I too hope to lose to God, even as my bones keep resisting, so that God's kingdom of love and justice will win in and around me. The practices of this book are about advancing this kingdom. We're not passive. It takes everything we have to keep practicing so that little by little we lose so we might win.

For the kingdom to come it's crucial we lose to God our claim of ownership. Then we can be faithful stewards of God's kingdom. I'll adapt a story from Professor Mark Allan Powell to illustrate this.[2]

Let's say I'm going out of town for a few weeks' vacation and my cat and a goldfish need care. I know a couple of responsible twenty-five-year-olds in town. They live in a cramped, sweaty studio apartment. So I invite them to housesit. It's good for them to spread out and have a real kitchen and air conditioning. It's good for me because my lawn will be cut and my pets will be fed.

If I come back after three weeks and everything is well taken care of and it worked out perfectly for everyone involved, then I'd say the housesitters were *good stewards* of my house.

But what if after three weeks I come back from vacation and the grass hasn't been mowed? Dozens of empty beer cans are scattered like aluminum leaves across the front lawn. I walk up to the door, open it and see the couch ruined with stains while the stink of decaying Chinese food hangs in the air. My precious goldfish, Goldy, is floating belly up. Well, the publishable thing I would say is, "They were *bad stewards* of my house."

Now for another scenario. What if I come back after three weeks and see that the front lawn is perfectly manicured? It's encouraging, but I'm still slightly nervous as I walk up and peek through a front window. The interior looks immaculate. Wonderful. Ready to go inside, I put my key to the lock, but it doesn't fit. After trying a few times, it's clear the lock has been changed. I look in the window again and notice the furniture is rearranged—some of the furniture isn't even mine. The fish tank has clean water, but there is a lion fish swimming in there and Goldy is nowhere in sight. And the twenty-five-year-olds are playing Xbox. I ring the doorbell and knock. They eventually glance at me, but wave their hands dismissively and then go back to their game like the house is now theirs.

In this case the biggest problem is not whether they were *good stewards* or *bad stewards*—it's that they forgot they were stewards at all. They think they're the *owners*.

We should hope to lose our claim to *ownership* in our wrestle with God and subsequently find the freedom to be the *faithful stewards* we are created to be. Then our lives and communities would look more like they should if God were king.

Through the five practices of this book, we are practicing, with our very lives, to become the answer to the prayer, *Thy kingdom come on earth as in heaven.* When I find the injustice around me or the failure to do these practices to be overwhelming, here are some simple, practical ways to keep moving forward.

• • •

Leave behind what holds you back. Discovering what holds us back in these practices can help us to improve at them. In Jesus' interaction with the rich young man, he told him to give all he had to the poor and follow him (Lk 18:18-29). What seems harsh at first is on closer reading an invitation of grace for us to remove what gets in the way of following the path of life and love. *Seek first [God's] kingdom and his righteousness, and all these things will be given to you as well,* Jesus said (Mt 6:33 NIV). He didn't say "Find first God's kingdom and then . . ." We seek, we don't always find, at least not right away and all at once. So we practice. It's hard but not thankless. As we seek, we're led into a meaningful life. That's what Jesus was inviting the rich young man to. And with these practices, step by step, we can find help in responding to Jesus' invitation.

Step forward with faith. Jesus watched a widow giving her two coins in the temple. Out of her poverty she gave all she had (Mk 12:41-44). As we practice justice, we're strengthened in our ability to live out of faith, to reorder priorities. *The kingdom of God belongs to those who are like little children,* Jesus said (Lk 18:15-17). Not to the powerful but to the vulnerable, the seeking, the learning, the wide-eyed, like the children and this widow. *The kingdom of heaven is like a treasure hidden in the field, which a man found and hid; and from joy over it he sells all that he has and buys that field* (Mt 13:44). We reject cheap compassion because we want something more real, more valuable, worth the kind of beautiful risk Jesus holds up. It's worth selling stock in the kingdom of self-interest so we can invest in the kingdom of God.

> **In our reliance on God we see that we are stewards, not owners.**

In our reliance on God we see that we are stewards, not owners. We don't have to force things in unhealthy ways or use shortcuts instead of patiently persisting together. We don't have to fear our lack of perfect knowledge. We are freed to be faithful, which is a lot of work, hard work, for a lifetime. But it's also freedom. We can be guided by faithfulness through practices that lead toward lasting change. This is the freedom of the epigraph at the opening of this book from Kierkegaard's *Purity of Heart Is to Will One Thing*:

He is not, therefore, eternally responsible for whether he reaches his goal within this world of time. But without exception, he is eternally responsible for the kind of means he uses.

And when he . . . only uses those means which are genuinely good, then, in the judgment of eternity, he is at the goal.[3]

Like the monk, we want to keep losing ourselves to God—so we're transformed into our best selves by God, who wants us to flourish as individuals and together. We are freed into faithfulness to step forward into the transformation of God's kingdom coming on earth.

Find opportunities for healing and reconciliation. Zacchaeus, a tax collector, exploited his power but then repented after an encounter with Jesus. Half his possessions he gave to the poor; to anyone he had cheated he paid back four times the amount (Lk 19:1-10). As we practice faithful justice, Zacchaeus reminds us to give for reconciliation with and for healing of the people we or others have exploited, or from whose exploitation we've benefited. The practices of attention and confession can lead us toward making things right. Jesus reveals that the *kingdom is coming* with this transformative encounter. Yes, even in the midst of our doubts, we have reason for hope. We seek to make our lives witnesses to this advancing of the kingdom, step by step.

Renew a vision of mutual flourishing. Jesus said if we have two of something (coats, enough food) and someone else doesn't have one, then give one away. We pay attention to the difference between *want* and *need* with the needs of our neighbors in mind. We still keep a needed jacket (*contra* the widow who gave everything), but not more than that. We can extrapolate from this that we can keep what we need to take care of our children, but not indulge them at the expense of other children who are going hungry. The specific choices are still hard to figure out, but the vision becomes revitalized and clearer through good partnering and truthing. *The kingdom of God is like a mustard seed*, Jesus said (Mt 13:31). It's important for us to practice justice and to have a vision for a kingdom in which we don't hoard but where everyone flourishes. The seed can be planted and grow beyond our own efforts. We'll be surprised at times by how very long it takes to grow into a tree. But we will also be surprised by joy as seeds grow into more than we could have ever hoped.

Find joy. As my colleague John Engle and I started our Haiti-focused nonprofit six years ago, we listed nine things that help explain who we want to be. These largely reflect the approach articulated in this book. But we also added a tenth: to work with people we laugh with.

We did this because we like working with fun people, but more importantly because joy can be a kind of lifeline as we work for justice, which exposes us to suffering and exacts a toll on us. A reminder of this toll is reflected in a 2013 study commissioned by the United Nations Commissioner for Refugees. The study found that 47 percent of its staff had sleep problems and 57 percent had recently experienced symptoms consistent with depression. In an article about this, former aid worker Rosalie Hughes cited "adult trauma exposure" as a main cause.[4]

Laughter of course doesn't solve this, and the article offers specific recommendations. But for me, it points toward the need for help and support if we want to practice faithfulness in kingdom work. Good support from friends, organizations or professional counselors can be important for moving to forgiveness and laughter that helps us stay in this for the long haul. As Paul says in the letter to the Romans, "The kingdom of God is not food and drink but righteousness and peace and joy in the

Holy Spirit. . . . Let us then pursue what makes for peace and for mutual upbuilding" (Rom 14:17, 19).

For this to happen we should expect a lot from each other in the work of the slow kingdom coming, but we also have to forgive each other a lot. Not forgiveness in the sense of ignoring problems or pretending they don't happen. We need forgiveness in the sense of wanting to be healed like the man in Bethsaida (Mk 8:22-26)—so we can keep a clear vision of partnering for healing with others, step by step.

I never liked the verse "the joy of the LORD is your strength" (Neh 8:10). It sounded too glib. It sounded like a superficial cliché chorus sung over and over and over again. Until recently. I'm starting to get it. Nehemiah says this during the tremendously demanding project of rebuilding Jerusalem. He spoke of that joy from God as a strength, not as escapism from sadness, but with each word wrung out of sweat and tears, out of callused hands from the commitment of a long, daunting project of rebuilding a destroyed city.

The work of justice, mercy and humility is hard stuff. Yet one of the fruits of stepping forward into faithful justice is the experience of joy and deep gladness.

● ● ●

We're vulnerable to death and to life. Jesus taught us to pray, *Do not bring us to the time of trial, but rescue us from the evil one* (Mt 6:13). We're vulnerable to wanting to claim the house like the housesitters at the beginning of this chapter. In a way, each of the five practices of this book are asking for us to not be tempted or to be saved from temptation.

The old monk in the story at the beginning of this chapter said he used to wrestle with the devil. God, rescue us from the evil one. Rescue us from times of temptation. Rescue us from complacency. Rescue us from the selfishness that harms us and others. Rescue us from blindness that makes it hard to see your kingdom coming. Rescue us from despair, that we would be resurrected by hope.

Yes, *to* resurrection. Don't just rescue us *from*. Resurrect us each day *to* faithfulness and *to* participating in your story of justice. Resurrect us each day to life, to abundant life. Unlike the old monk, I still wrestle plenty with temptations. But like the old monk, the work of justice can often feel like we're wrestling with God, where we hope God will win: Come, Lord Jesus, come.

As I was finishing the last few pages of this book, I attended Margaret's funeral. A hundred people came to mourn her passing and celebrate her ninety-two years of life, which seemed to involve wrestling both with the devil and God to the end. She's the kind of person who shows that even if I live fifty more years, I'm pretty sure that's not nearly enough time for the Spirit, even on overtime, to make me as good and kind a person as Margaret.

We saw Margaret regularly at church. She was also a volunteer, supporter and encourager for my work in Haiti. In her late eighties she would come to sell tickets at our education events and get into the nitty gritty of helping. But as amazing as I thought she was, I only knew a fraction before her funeral.

At her funeral I learned her parents had both been alcoholics. According to an article read at the service, her mother was "a fall down drunk" and her dad "a functional drunk." At a young age she vowed she would never drink. Nevertheless, she started to drink in college, then couldn't stop. Even with a professional job and being a mom, she couldn't stop. Then fifty-six years ago her life was transformed by Christ; she stopped drinking and began working for God's kingdom. She started a halfway house for thirty-eight men, then a halfway house for twenty women in the

Springfield, Massachusetts, area. Later she was part of starting a detox center, which was named after her. She paid attention to where she could help, confessed daily her vulnerability and reliance on God, showed a profound respect in how she treated people, and in the past ten years, when I knew her, she was a generous partner in helping people toward sobriety and in other ways. Even as she was dying in hospice, her focus was asking about others at church and wanting to hear how students in Haiti were doing.

No, the kingdom didn't fully come in Margaret's lifetime. Not even close. We have an achingly long way to go. But the kingdom did come in her. During the funeral we sang the hymn "Here I Am, Lord," which echoes the prophet Isaiah's response to God's call on his life. Isaiah confessed his unworthiness, then responded with faithful action to the responsibilities given to him (Is 6). The kingdom coming changed Margaret's life and then changed the lives of many around her. Margaret responded to God's call by faithfully doing justice, loving mercy and walking humbly.

In addition to thinking about Margaret, her funeral made me reflect on gratitude for the very gift of life and grace. Gratitude for my family and friends; for colleagues who I've learned so much from, in many countries, over many years; for the chance to help someone get an opportunity she wouldn't otherwise have. Gratitude for so many who have given me opportunities; for connections with people across cultures; for being welcomed into people's lives; for so many inspiring, generous people,

> **Gratitude, like joy, is essential fuel for faithfulness.**

because I need inspiration (breath) again and again; for the mysterious presence of grace; and for the gritty working out of love.

I see in others and in myself that gratitude, like joy, is essential fuel for faithfulness. Anger is important and just, but alone it can turn to bitterness and cause us to corrode. Self-righteousness can work for a while but will exhaust us and everyone around us. Gratitude can burn bright and long toward making a lasting difference. Gratitude cultivates joy and can help sustain us through the inevitable failures. Gratitude often seems very much like faith, which leads us to practice *attention, confession, respect, partnering* and *truthing*. And we keep practicing.

In the first chapter we read about Alicia, who still supports Belyse for thirty dollars every month. She doesn't love how all the stories about Belyse are presented, but she's happy to keep helping her. She also started giving to another charity that is transparent about how her money is used in a Kenyan community. She started volunteering at a neighborhood school that was and is discriminated against. It was unsettling to step into this painful racial history. But one morning Alicia realized that her compassion needed *heart* and *truthing*. She's reading, giving and voting differently. She's getting more out of her community and feeling more accountable to her community too. The boy she tutors weekly sometimes bangs the table in frustration. With Skittles and a lot of encouragement, they make it through together. She's experiencing the kingdom coming, ever so slowly, from a distance and up close.

Sam kept reflecting on his experience through university. He became a history major, with a focus on American history. Then he decided to go to law school. After he graduated, he worked for a high-powered firm. He thought he'd learn a lot and make a lot of money to pay off student loans and be able to give a lot of money. But after a few years he realized it was like high school again, where he was living in a different world of privilege that fostered a kind of complacency. His *attention* awoke again and he quit the firm and joined a small law firm in his hometown. He does some corporate work, but mostly works for reduced fees and pro bono to prevent evictions and help small businesses through legal issues. He goes to at least a few of his school's basketball games every year, where he sits with other guys he was on the team with. They reminisce about the glory days when they could run and jump. They talk like they'd still be able to get out there and beat these youngsters, but know they couldn't. He feels a lot of sadness for the problems still in his community, but likes how his ambitions have been turned around and upside down. Faithfulness is uncomfortable at times, but overall he feels a deep freedom and gladness.

First Church stopped flirting and using other people as "experiences." They found freedom in starting to practice *attention*, much like Calvary Church in Michigan. First Church just completed a sixth trip to Guatemala. The change wasn't easy. They found, through *truthing*, that the English-speaking pastor they had originally partnered with in Guatemala talked charismatically about Jesus with them but wasn't a good leader in the community. They *confessed* as a church that they had partnered in a way that was easy instead of thoughtful. It burst the heroic narrative they'd been telling themselves. It's hard to lose innocence, but their experience has led to a deeper, more mature hope. They're into a strong partnership with an organization that monitors what is happening and helps them to be culturally sensitive. They're discovering more than they'd ever known about their own privilege and assumptions. The relationship isn't as giddy as a series of first dates, but it feels real, like marriage.

The small team that started an orphanage are humbled by failure but are now free to practice *respect* and *partnering* as apprentices, which has turned things around. They learn from the mistakes of others rather than repeating them. Their new insights are less grand but make more difference. They're working with another organization to place children in Cambodian foster care families, with good support and rigorous accountability. It's not as glamorous, but now they want the zeal of faith to be guided by wisdom. They're inspired by the young people, both Cambodians and Americans, they get to work with.

Meanwhile Yanique is practicing faithfulness instead of obeying ideals. They often look the same, but faithful love is ultimately what liberates. She's learned to *confess* her mixed motives and to receive grace in her search. It's not about fear or other people's expectations anymore. She has been involved with Black Lives Matter locally and gathered a few friends to go to rallies in other cities. She's working for a community development organization that has a mix of public and private funding, that does some for-profit and some nonprofit work. She keeps *truthing* to find the best ways she can help—and she's found freedom to faithfully participate in change that will last.

• • •

The title *Slow Kingdom Coming* is for me a lament: we confess that we long for change and we long for it to come sooner, with continuous tears like that weeping willow tree in the chapter on confession. *Slow Kingdom Coming* is also a commitment: we see the need for faithful ways that avoid shortcuts and live out the vision of the kingdom each step along the way, that we would be transformed and be part of transformative work. And, finally, *Slow Kingdom Coming* is a declaration of hope. It's not here yet, but we believe and are willing to give our lives to living out this belief.

More than twenty years ago, when I was in college, a few friends and I would get together once a week to read the Bible or a book and pray in a small, seldom-used chapel room on the second floor of our student center. We spent a lot more time on the ground floor playing foosball and Ping-Pong, but up in that quiet room, one of the books we read was *The Imitation of Christ* by Thomas à Kempis. In it he says, "Fight bravely, for habit overcomes habit."[5]

Yes, that is the hope and the work and the promise. We don't have to be perfect, but we are invited, in the most meaningful commitment of our lives, to *practice bravely* because it leads to deep change.

Thomas à Kempis was writing in the fifteenth century about our inner, spiritual lives, but this same encouragement applies to practicing faithful

> **We are invited to practice bravely because it leads to deep change.**

justice. Practice bravely because habit overcomes habit. Practice bravely because practicing will shape the world in and around you as you do justice, love mercy and walk humbly in the world.

Our world can crush us under compassion or turn us callous. This is another way. We can't be perfect. We can't meet all the needs around us. But we can practice following, step by step.

Jesus' invitation can be received as grace. More than grace, though, right? It's also an invitation to life itself, a life of love, truth and justice. It's an invitation to kick at the darkness. It's an invitation to weep at the world but then get up, wipe the tears from our eyes and see a little more clearly the vision for this kingdom coming and how we can help it to come.

From the outset we've seen how these five practices attend both to our inner life and to our outward actions. *The kingdom of God is among you,* Jesus said (Lk 17:20-21). The kingdom grows in the world like a tree, which we watch after planting a seed; it also grows within our spirits and actions.

In the preface, I said I'd be good with skipping God's blessing if we could get a little extra help changing things around here. But this whole book actually is saying that the blessing is, in fact, that we do get to participate with God in making this change happen. We very much need this kind of blessing. So let's end— or, hopefully, let's begin—with a variation of the beautiful benediction from the book of Numbers:

May God bless you
> *so you may deeply know that blessing and bless others.*

May God keep you
> *so as you know God's embrace you then reach out to embrace others.*

May God's face shine upon you
> *so you may experience with others the warm light of creating together with God.*

May God be gracious to you
> *so our practices of justice don't feel like rules but like freedom and joy.*

May God's face turn toward you
> *so you know you aren't left to do this alone.*

May God give you peace
> *so step by step we practice moving together toward the flourishing of God's kingdom.*

APPENDIX

Study Guides, Resources and
How These Five Practices Work Together

GROUP STUDY GUIDES

There are two group study guides prepared for you—one for a single session on the book and another for extended study over six weeks. Both are free and available at kentannan.com.

RESOURCES

I've pulled together more resources for you to look at, including websites, books, interviews and more stories. They're also available on my website.

HOW THESE PRACTICES WORK TOGETHER

Throughout the book I talk about how the practices are related. But here in the appendix I also want to share in more detail several ways these practices can work together. These aren't the only ways to use the practices; you can apply them however they are most beneficial to you. But I hope the following will be helpful to some people and groups for applying these practices in your work and life.

Sequential. I ordered the five practices in a way that makes sequential sense. Often our *attention* is first awoken to injustice and wanting to make a difference. Then there is an element of *confession* as we become aware of our own vulnerabilities and longing for change. Then as we enter into the work of justice with people, *respect* should guide us. This allows us to move into *partnering,* in which we participate as equal agents in each others' flourishing. Finally, as we're faithful to God, with these practices helping, our desire to be faithful leads us to *truthing* so we can be good stewards in our efforts to help others.

This use can be especially helpful when starting a new project or ministry, launching a new organization or taking on a new personal volunteer opportunity.

Repeating cycle. Often, after we finish that sequence, we quickly see how we can start the cycle again. That is, once we move through the five practices in our reflections and our actions, we're naturally led from truthing right back to attention, because truthing helps us to find new answers and ask new questions. So we're led back to attention with new eyes, which leads us to being aware of and then confessing things we hadn't even realized before. From there, we can move into respect and partnering that are more sensitive and focused. Our truthing then addresses new questions at the aerial level, and we've become better at understanding our experiences on the ground. And then, well, then we get to start all over again.

At least that's the way it is for me. These practices keep building on one another for me and with colleagues. They're never done. We keep going around the cycle, hitting dead ends sometimes, learning, failing (fortunately, confession is one of the practices) and then cycling through these practices so we can keep participating together in the coming of God's kingdom.

Random reinforcing. I also find there are seasons of growth in one of the practices more than others. For example, I have an experience on a trip, a conversation with a colleague, read an article, hear about the work someone else is doing or discover a new idea that calls our attention to truthing for a few weeks. Ultimately that reinforces our ability to respect others because we've found a better way to listen through analyzing the impact of our work. Or a conversation with a friend reveals, uncomfortably, my need to confess, and then confessing opens me up to partnering in a more trusting way.

My experience is that growing in any of these practices will reinforce and deepen the others.

Evaluation and opportunity grid. I hope these practices will help you evaluate your volunteering, a church's ministry, an organization's justice work or who you decide to support with your time, talents and money. How are these five practices being applied? Is respect being shown? Is there truthing that reveals the importance of trying to be fruitful with good ideas and good work on the ground, rather than reducing work to mere statistics? What is the approach to partnership? Is there sufficient attention to what is happening to people so they won't be burned out but are working on what is important and in a way that they'll be able to do it for the long term?

A friend of mine had read an early copy of this book before he went on a trip with friends and extended family. Each day on this trip they visited a different ministry. After each visit, my friend found these practices helpful as a way to debrief and think through what they found good about the justice work in each place. The practices are also a helpful grid for evaluating important areas to change or grow. Just because people are doing justice or missionary work doesn't mean we can't ask them questions. Actually, I always find that questions like these from supporters are good and important. They help to keep us accountable and growing. So these practices can be used as evaluation tools.

In the work I do, I apply the practices in this way. I also use the practices to think about how I engage justice, and even how I'm doing as a dad and husband. Maybe they're part of a weekly review. Or they can be helpful to guide thinking about life, work and helping other people. Maybe they're part of planning for your new year and articulating where your hopes are for engaging in justice and growing spiritually.

Individually or together. I find these practices encouraging. They're also hard. My wife is better at attention than I am. I chase new ideas. She's great at sticking to the important ideas and keeping herself and others moving toward them in ways that serve everyone and the big picture. I have a couple of colleagues who are better than I am at truthing because they have the training and minds to track data and evaluate it meticulously. So I find all five of these practices personally important, but then in our organization or our church I'm grateful we have a diversity of gifts.

People are stronger in some practices than others. So we rely on, learn from and sharpen each other. We participate in and practice for the slow kingdom coming as individuals and together.

With grace. These five practices also work together by grace. "Thy kingdom come on earth as in heaven" is of course a prayer, which illuminates our calling, but it also signals our reliance on God. We need God's grace to do justice, love mercy and walk humbly with God and neighbor. We need grace to help us in all of these practices. (My family and colleagues could all too easily let you know how much grace I need as I try to live these.) This doesn't reduce our responsibility to do them well and to keep improving, but we do need grace.

My wife's uncle recently told me about attending an elementary school music recital. A girl in second or third grade got up to sing. She stood, slightly nervous, alone on stage. She started to sing a cappella. A few lines in the song started to go down the scale and it became clear she hadn't started high enough. She couldn't hit the low notes. She realized her mistake and stopped.

The audience tensed, breathless, expecting her to start crying or run off the stage.

Instead she stood there silently, looking straight ahead, collecting herself. Then she started—on a higher note—to sing again. She sang beautifully through to the end. Standing ovation.

We learn by failing. Like that girl in the recital, we can fail well and keep learning as part of truthing and faithfulness. We don't have to be perfect; we get to keep responding to God's call. We keep practicing.

With truthing. I hope these practices can become part of your reflection and action. I also know there is room to sharpen these, add more examples and learn from the perspective and experiences of others. Part of walking humbly in the world is giving our very best and then knowing that others can correct or improve on it. Many different people, places, cultures and experiences have shaped me, but I'm still writing from my limited perspective.

So I hope these practices are the beginning of conversations that will help you work them out in your context. The practice of truthing applies also to taking a book like this and then working it out with your feet on the ground (and hopefully avoiding alligators).

● ● ●

For more tools and information on *Slow Kingdom Coming*, and to share your experiences and insights, please visit kentannan.com.

ACKNOWLEDGMENTS

Mom and Dad, you first taught me about the kingdom coming, and I dedicate this book to you with much love and gratitude.

Partnering is one of the five practices I highlighted, and this book was only possible because of many partnerships.

I've worked with and learned from so many great people over the past twenty-two years. I'm especially grateful to our Haiti Partners team in Haiti, the United States and Canada. Special thanks to John Engle, Jonathan Chan, and Enel Angervil for shaping my thinking in this book. I'm also grateful for the chance to learn with the team at the Equitas Group: Lance Robinson, Andy Crouch, Jena Nardella, Jonathan Scoonover and Jeremy Floyd. The Sunday school class at Our Savior helped with feedback on early drafts, and Norm and Sandy Stevenson gave special encouragement.

For each person who has supported the work I've been involved in over the years, I've been so grateful, humbled and honored to partner with you.

I'm grateful to InterVarsity's entire talented and dedicated team: Helen Lee was an insightful and encouraging editor who guided and improved the book significantly—and who I loved learning from. Drew Blankman's copyediting sharpened it. Jeff Crosby helped plant the seed for the book and encouraged me along the way.

I'm also thankful for help from Dave Zimmerman and Doug Davidson. Aaron LeClaire, Adrianna Wright, Tony Lin and Laura Seay strengthened it through their smart and generous feedback.

Kathy Helmers is a wonderful agent and partner who I love getting to work with. I'm very grateful for her guidance.

I'm thankful to and inspired by the people whose stories I got to share in the book.

It's standard but important to say I'm to blame for anything that has gone awry. I should also say my gratitude extends to many people beyond this page.

Finally, I'm especially grateful to the people I'm closest to and with whom I get to live, in my stumbling way, into the kingdom coming: Shelly, Simone and Cormac. Thank you, thank you, thank you. I love you deeply.

NOTES

Participating in the Coming Kingdom

[1]Louis C. K., "Everything's Amazing and Nobody's Happy," *Late Night with Conan O'Brien*, Episode 15.169, October 1, 2008.

[2]John Bunyan, *The Pilgrim's Progress* (London: David Bogue, 1850), 18.

[3]Walter Brueggemann, "Moses, Pharoah, the Prophets and Us," *Embracing the Prophets*, session 1 (Morehouse Education Resources, January 2012), DVD.

Attention: Awakening to Justice

[1]Mark Barden as quoted by Rachel Marie Stone, "Sandy Hook dad on what you can do right now to prevent violence," *Religious News Service*, June 26, 2014, www.rachelmariestone.religionnews.com/2014/06/26/sandy-hook-dad-can-right-now-help-prevent-violence.

[2]For more information on Open Space, go to www.openspaceworld.org.

[3]Simone Weil, "Reflections on the Right Use of School Studies with a View to the Love of God," in *Waiting for God* (New York: G. P. Putnam's Sons, 1951), 57-66.

[4]Ibid.

Confession: The Posture for Engaging

[1]Søren Kierkegaard, *Papers and Journals* (New York: Penguin, 2015), loc. 2789.

[2]U2, "One," *Achtung Baby*, 1991.

[3]Kent Annan, *After Shock* (Downers Grove, IL: InterVarsity Press, 2011), 52.

[4]Fredrick Buechner, *Wishful Thinking* (New York: Harper & Row, 1973), 95.

[5]Bruce Wydick, "The Impact of TOMS Shoes," *Across Two Worlds* (blog), March 16, 2015, www.acrosstwoworlds.net/?p=292. This article refers to a study Wydick and others contributed to for the *Journal of Development Effectiveness*.

[6]Diogenes Allen, *Spiritual Theology* (Lanham, MD: Cowley, 1997), 76.

[7]Robert J. Priest and Joseph Paul Priest, "They See Everything and Understand Nothing," *Missiology: An International Review* 36, no. 1 (January 2008): 53-73.

[8]Martin Luther King Jr., "Where Do We Go from Here?," in *A Testament of Hope: The Essential Writings and Speeches of Martin Luther King, Jr.*, ed. James M. Washington (New York: HarperCollins, 1986), 252.

[9]See www.onechurchliturgy.com.

RESPECT: THE GOLDEN RULE FOR HELPING

[1]See Bruce Wydick, "The Impact of TOMS Shoes," *Across Two Worlds* (blog), March 16, 2015, www.acrosstwoworlds.net/?p=292 for an example of research asking these kinds of questions.

[2]For an international study on this topic, see Kim Yi Dionne, "Local Demand for a Global Intervention: Policy Priorities in the Time of AIDS," *World Development* 40, no. 12 (2012): 2468-77.

[3]N. T. Wright, "Paul, Arabia, and Elijah (Galatians 1:17)," *Journal of Biblical Literature* 115, no. 4 (1996): 689.

[4]Dietrich Bonhoeffer, *The Cost of Discipleship* (New York: Touchstone, 1995), 44-45.

[5]Martin Luther King Jr., "Strive Toward Freedom," in *A Testament of Hope: The Essential Writings of Martin Luther King, Jr.*, ed. James M. Washington (New York: HarperCollins, 1991), 417-90.

[6]Author interview with William Easterly, "Poverty Is a Moral Problem," *Christianity Today* (web only), April 2, 2014, www.christianitytoday.com/ct/2014/april-web-only/poverty-is-moral-problem.html.

[7]Robert Woodberry, "The Missionary Roots of Liberal Democracy," *American Political Science Review* 106, no. 2 (2012): 244-74.

PARTNERING: *WITH* NOT *FOR*

[1]I told some of Enel's story in my book *After Shock,* including how he survived being on the third floor of a six-floor building that collapsed in Haiti's 2010 earthquake.

[2]For more about this period of Haiti's history see Laurent Dubois, *Haiti: The Aftershocks of History* (New York: Metropolitan, 2012).

[3]Eugene Peterson, *The Contemplative Pastor* (Grand Rapids: Eerdmans, 1989), 120.

[4]See Gary A. Haugen, *Good News About Injustice,* 10th anniversary ed. (Downers Grove, IL: InterVarsity Press, 2009); and *Just Courage* (Downers Grove, IL: InterVarsity Press, 2008).

TRUTHING: HARD THINKING AND FEET ON THE GROUND

[1]George Orwell, *In Front of Your Nose 1946-1950,* ed. Sonia Orwell and Ian Angus (Boston: Nonpareil Books, 2000), 125.

[2]Christopher Blattman and Paul Niehaus, "Show Them the Money," *Foreign Affairs,* May-June 2014, www.foreignaffairs.com/articles/show -them-money.

[3]The Thriving Cities project is through the Institute of Advanced Studies at the University of Virginia.

[4]David Foster Wallace, *Infinite Jest* (New York: Back Bay Books, 2006), 378.

[5]Diogenes Allen, *Three Outsiders: Pascal, Kierkegaard, Simone Weil* (Eugene, OR: Wipf & Stock, 2006), 38-39. See also Blaise Pascal, "Of the Need of Seeking Truth," in *The Thoughts of Blaise Pascal* (London: G. Bell and Sons, 1905), 94-95.

PRACTICING FAITHFULLY EVEN WHEN WE'RE OVERWHELMED

[1]Nikos Kazantzakis, *Report to Greco,* trans. P. A. Bien (New York: Touch-stone, 1975), loc. 3531.

[2]Mark Allan Powell, *Biblical Stewardship: Our Duty and Delight* (Select Learning), video series.

[3]Søren Kierkegaard, *Purity of Heart Is to Will One Thing* (Seaside, OR: Rough Draft, 2014), 143.

[4]Rosalie Hughes, "A Crisis of Anxiety Among Aid Workers," *New York Times*, March 8, 2015, www.nytimes.com/2015/03/09/opinion/a-crisis -of-anxiety-among-aid-workers.html?_r=0.

[5]Thomas à Kempis, *The Imitation of Christ*, ed. William C. Creasy (Macon, GA: Mercer University Press, 2007), chap. 21.

ABOUT THE AUTHOR

Kent Annan is a writer, speaker and codirector of Haiti Partners, a nonprofit focused on education in Haiti. He received his master of divinity from Princeton Theological Seminary.

He is the author of *Slow Kingdom Coming*, *After Shock*, and *Following Jesus Through the Eye of the Needle*. His writing has also appeared in many magazines and literary journals. He has spent numerous years working with people in difficult situations around the world, including with refugees in Europe and with people in Haiti for the past thirteen years.

Kent is on the board of directors of Equitas Group, a philanthropic foundation focused on ending child exploitation in Haiti and Southeast Asia. He teaches adult education in his local church and speaks regularly to groups around the country.

Kent, his wife, Shelly, his daughter, Simone, and his son, Cormac, live in Florida.

ALSO BY KENT ANNAN

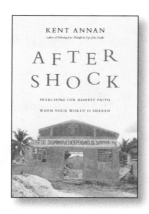

After Shock
Searching for Honest Faith When Your World Is Shaken

Following Jesus Through the Eye of the Needle
Living Fully, Loving Dangerously